The Morning S

S0-EGQ-419

Vol 1 No 2 ♦ JOURNAL ♦ $2.95

Editors: Rick Joyner and Francis Frangipane
Contributing Editors: Dudley Hall, DeVerne Fromke
Managing Editor: Angie Thompson
Design/Production: Angie Thompson
Copy Editors: Julie Joyner, Stewart Spencer

The Morning Star Journal is a publication of MorningStar Publications of Pineville, North Carolina.

MorningStar Publications is a non-profit organization dedicated to the promulgation of important teachings and timely prophetic messages to the church. We also attempt to promote interchange between the different streams, emphases and denominations in the body of Christ.

Subscriptions. To receive a subscription to ***The Morning Star*** Journal, send payment along with your name and address to MorningStar Publications, Post Office Box 369, Pineville, NC 28134. One year (6 bi-monthly issues) US $10.00; outside US $17.50. Prices are subject to change without notice. (See next page for bulk subscription information.)

Reprints. Photocopies of any part of the contents of this publications may be made freely. To re-typeset information, however, permission must be requested in writing from MorningStar Publications, Post Office Box 369, Pineville, NC 28134.

Letters. Direct all correspondance to the address below. Contributions are tax deductible. Your support is appreciated.

MorningStar Publications
P.O. Box 369 • Pineville, NC 28134

♦ ♦

TEACHING

♦ ♦

INTERCESSION

♦ ♦

PROPHECY

The Morning Star

♦ JOURNAL ♦

♦ ♦

WORSHIP

♦ ♦

FAMILY

♦ ♦

STUDIES

♦ ♦

DIRECTORY

A Time To Seek God

by Francis Frangipane

"When Thou didst say, 'Seek My face,' my heart said to Thee, 'Thy face, O Lord, I shall seek'" (Psalm 27:8).
(King David)

There are certain times when the Lord calls us out of the routine of our daily lives into a special season when His only command is: "Seek My face." This is when He has something precious and vital to give us that the familiar pattern of our daily devotions cannot accommodate. During such times people are often delivered of sins that have plagued them for years; others discover a depth in their walk with God that leads to greater effectiveness in ministry and prayer; still others experience breakthroughs in their families and are used by God to see loved ones brought into the Kingdom.

Yet, here we are not to seek God for things or even for other people, but for God Himself. Maturity starts as we break the cycle of seeking God only during hardship and begin to seek Him because we love Him and want to know Him. A touch from God is wonderful, but we are in pursuit of more than just experience—more than "goose bumps and tears." *We are seeking to abide with Christ, where we are continually aware of His fullness within us, where His Presence dwells in us in glory.*

How do we enter this sacred place? If we study the life of Moses, we will see how he sought God and lived in fellowship with Him:

> Now Moses used to take the tent and pitch it outside the camp, a good distance from the camp, and he called it the tent of meeting. And it came about, that everyone who sought the Lord would go out to the tent of meeting which was outside the camp (Exodux 33:7).

Notice that, "everyone who sought the Lord would go out." If we are going to truly seek the Lord, we must **"go out"** as did Moses and those who sought the Lord. We must pitch our tent **"a good distance from the camp."** What camp is this? For Moses, as well as for us, it is the "camp of familiarity."

Is there anything inherently wrong or sinful with the things that are familiar? No, not in themselves, but you will remember that when Jesus told His disciples to follow Him, He called them to leave the familiar pattern of their lives for extended periods and be alone with Him (Matthew 19:27, Luke 14:33). Why? Because He knew that men, by nature, are unconsciously governed by the familiar. If He was to expand us to receive the eternal, He would have to rescue us from the limitations of the temporal.

This is not to say we should neglect our families, or that we become irresponsible as we seek God. No. God has given everyone enough time to seek Him. It is there. Having done what love would have us do for our families, we simply say no to every other voice but God's. We must redeem the time: cancel hobbies, forsake television, put away the newspaper and magazines. Those who really desire to find God will find time.

Sadly, many Christians have no higher goal, no greater aspiration, than to become "normal."

Their desires are limited to measuring up to others. Without a true vision of God, we most certainly will perish spiritually! Paul rebuked the church at Corinth because they walked, "...like mere men" (I Corinthians 3:3). God has more for us than merely becoming better people; He wants to flood our lives with the same power that raised Christ from the dead!

We must understand: God does not want us "normal," He wants us Christlike! For the Holy Spirit to facilitate God's purposes in our lives, He must redefine both our definition of reality and our priorities in life. Christlikeness must become our singular goal.

For most people, however, our sense of reality, and hence, our security, is oftentimes rooted in the familiar. How difficult it is to grow spiritually if our security is based upon the stability of outward things! Our security must come from God, not circumstances, not even relationships. A true Christian's sense of reality needs to be rooted in Christ. When it is, the other areas of his life experience eternal security.

Yet, our fears run deep and are numerous. Indeed, most of us pass through life umbilically tied to the protection of the familiar. Experience tells us that many good people remain in lifeless churches simply because they desire the security of familiar faces more than the truth of Christ. Even people who have been delivered from adverse situations are often drawn back into hardship. Why? *Because adversity is more familiar to them.* Consider that certain prisoners are repeat offenders simply because they are more accustomed to prison life than freedom. Is it not true that, often, young girls who have been abused by their fathers, tend to seek out and marry men who eventually abuse them as their fathers did? Groping blindly through life, they sought the familiar. It is significant that, worldwide, most people live within fifty miles of their birthplaces.

Humans are cocooned, insulated against change by the familiar. When we work all day only to come home, watch television, then collapse in bed, our lifestyle becomes a chain of bondage. These things may not necessarily trap us in sin as much as they keep us from God.

Moses had to leave what was familiar and pitch his tent "outside the camp," in order to seek the Lord. "Therefore Jesus also, that He might sanctify the people through His own blood, suffered outside the gate. Hence, let us go out to Him outside the camp, bearing His reproach. For here we do not have a lasting city, but we are seeking the city which is to come" (Hebrews 13:12-14).

In the same way that Moses and those who sought the Lord went outside the camp, and as Jesus went outside the camp, so also must we, at times, leave the camp of what seems normal and predictable and begin to seek after God. Here we do not have a lasting city, but we are seeking the city which is to come.

This is one reason why Jesus said, "...when you pray, go into your inner room, and when you have shut your door, pray..." (Matthew 6:6). *Christ desires us to leave the familiar, distracting world of our senses and abide in the world of our hearts, bearing in mind that the highest goal of prayer is to find God.*

Every minute you seek God is a minute enriched with new life, new power from God. Give yourself a minimum amount of time—an hour or two each day, but do not set a limit, as the Lord may draw you to seek Him on into the night. And continue day by day, and week by week, until you have drawn near enough to God that you can hear His voice, becoming confident that He is close enough to you to hear your whisper (James 4:8).

To become a holy, sanctified people we must sever the chains, the restraints, the bondage of the familiar, the average life of "mere men." We must leave the camp of familiarity and place our tent in the Presence of God. ■

Do We REALLY BELIEVE In The RESURRECTION?

harles Spurgeon once made the remarkable statement that "There are very few Christians who believe in the resurrection." When I first read that statement I thought it was a misprint. How could someone be a Christian and not believe in the resurrection? As I pondered this I knew that there was truth to Spurgeon's statement. There is a difference between giving intellectual and doctrinal assent to the fact of the resurrection and having faith in it. There is a big difference between believing in our minds and believing in our hearts. *If we really believed in our hearts the truth of the resurrection our lives would be radically different.*

BY RICK JOYNER

The delusion that mere intellectual agreement with certain biblical and historical facts is true faith has caused many to feel safe in a spiritual condition in which their eternal lives may still be in jeopardy. As the apostle Paul made clear:

> ...if you confess with your mouth Jesus as Lord *and believe in your **heart*** that God raised Him from the dead, you shall be saved; for with *the **heart*** man believes, resulting in righteousness (Romans 10:9-10).

Funk & Wagnals Standard Handbook of Synonyms, Antonyms & Prepositions defines ***faith*** as "a union of belief and trust; *it is a belief so strong that it becomes a part of one's own nature.*" This is not to imply that Funk & Wagnals have authority to establish doctrine, but I believe this definition of faith is accurate according to biblical truth.

Faith is stronger than belief. To believe is to give intellectual assent; to have faith is to be inseparable from the object of your devotion. Belief can be changed or lost by a more persuasive argument; true faith is so much a part of the person it can only be taken by death. Faith is the substance of our very existence and identity; our faith is who we are. The stronger the faith of the believer, the stronger his existence and the more impact he will have. The more positive the faith, the more edifying this impact will be on the world and himself.

This difference between "belief" and "faith" is the difference between being true and a mere pretender who has deluded himself in order to appease his conscience. The popular and pervasive "believing in God," that is just believing that He exists, accomplishes little and is not the true Christian "faith." The concept that we just need to believe that He exists is a delusion that keeps us from the true religion of *faith in God.*

A person without true faith is like a car without an engine; it may have a beautiful appearance but it will not get you anywhere. The stronger the faith the further and the faster you will go. Belief alone is superficial and accomplishes little more than appeasing one's emotions. Faith is a living power that can move the mountains that stand in the way of it goal.

Moses led Israel into the wilderness in order to convert their superstitions and shallow beliefs into a rock solid faith. Your wilderness, the trials you are enduring to test your faith, is meant to accomplish the same for you. If you respond properly to your wilderness it will turn mere emotional frivolity into a force! Embrace your difficulties as opportunities and you *will* get to your promised land. Let the difficulties discourage you and you too will perish in that place and never realize your goal and purpose in the Lord.

Moses could lead Israel out of Egypt but he could not take the Egypt out of the Israelites; the difficulties of the wilderness were meant to do that. The Israelites had been slaves in Egypt; slavery is the most base human condition but there is a security therein which is hard to escape. Even though the Israelites were freed and moving toward their destiny and fulfillment, when they encountered difficulties most of them began looking back on the terrible oppression of slavery and wanted to return to it, feeling that they had been better off in Egypt!

This is the dividing line that separates those who go on to victory from those who go back to their doom. No one will attain his goal or destiny until he becomes *free.* The free man would rather perish in the wilderness trying to fulfill his destiny than go back to slavery. Until we make the decision that we will not go back, regardless of how painful it gets, we will not go forward. Jesus once declared, "No one who puts his hand to the plow, and then looks back, is fit for the kingdom of heaven" (Luke 9:62) If we are still looking back we are not ready to go forward.

The most telltale symptom of surrender to slavery is **grumbling** and **complaining.** The one who complains has lost the faith; he has already given up in his heart. The one with true faith meets even the most severe obstacles as an opportunity to win a greater victory and make a greater advance toward his goal. This cannot be blind optimism which is just another form of mere intellectual assessment masquerading as the true faith. Optimism will wither in the heat of the desert wilderness; true faith becomes stronger and more determined as the heat is increased.

Faith is able to move mountains and it will move every one that stands in its way; it will not even bother to go around them. True faith makes the road; it does not follow one. That is why true faith is true freedom; *no* shackle can be put on it. True faith is the ability to seize the vision of one's destiny with such a grip that it cannot be taken away until it is fulfilled. Such faith moves every obstacle, but is moved by no obstacle. True faith *will* get to the promised land.

The Israelites began to complain when they finally came to a well and found the waters to be bitter. They did not understand that God intended to turn the bitter waters into sweet as an object lesson. Their first response to the disappointment was doubt and complaining and by that the destroyer was released among them. Everyone who has been truly thirsty can identify with the Israelites. Real thirst arouses our basic instincts to survive. They may have had a real excuse to complain but this difficult test was also their greatest opportunity. It is the real test that brings out real faith. True faith is internal, not external and it is not dependent on external circumstances. True faith is not altered by disappointment; instead it is strengthened. It will always turn the bitter waters of disappointment into the sweet waters of opportunity. When disappointment results in complaining the destroyer of our faith has been released and our vision will become clouded.

> True faith is the ability to seize the vision of one's destiny with such a grip that it cannot be taken away until it is fulfilled.

Let us understand one important fact about true faith: true faith *is not* a faith in one's faith! True faith has an Object and a Source of its power which is greater than oneself. *True faith is not in the quality of our faith; true faith is in God!* Anything less is worse than a pretension; it is deception. Inevitably, those whose faith is in themselves only accomplish that which is selfish. Self-centeredness has proven to be a wide door to deception. The Bible astutely settles this issue at the beginning; when Adam and Eve, after listening to Satan's advice and ate of the forbidden fruit, the first fruit of their sin was that they immediately began to focus upon themselves and noticed their own nakedness. The self-centered are the most emotionally crippled, not to mention boring, mere shells of what the human being is meant to be. When we start looking to ourselves we will fall from the grace and power of true faith.

Finding that *Reason* for our lives, which is to find the mind of God, is the Object and Source of all true faith. Anything less than seeking the Purpose that is *ordained* is subhuman and not worthy of intelligent expenditure of energy or time. Only when we find *God's* plan and possess it with the true faith will we be fulfilled. This is the brilliance of the apostle who exhorted us to "study to show yourselves approved unto God," *not men*. When we have direction which we know is from the Source, a power is released called *faith* that nothing in the rest of creation can stand in the way of. There is no greater motivation than knowing our destiny, and there is no power available greater than that which is found in the resolve of those who are seizing their destiny.

Sadly, one of the greatest obstacles to understanding and believing the Christian faith has been the church. This is because much of the visible church has become an example of how shallow belief continually tries to usurp the position of true faith. The faith of the apostles was devoted to building a temple for God that could not be made with human hands; it could only be contained in human hearts. The church they preached was made of people who had the true faith. The church they preached about was not an organization but a living organism; it was not an institution but a constitution. The apostolic vision was God living in people—not bricks. When one grasps the true faith he does not go to church; *he becomes the church.* The true church is a source of power and life that no building or institution can contain—only the human heart is great enough when it has been purified by faith.

Reality is not found in ritual. True faith is a

river of life too powerful to be contained in the pitiful little structures in which weak visioned men have tried to keep it. There are certainly gatherings of those who share a real faith and the power of that faith, and *some* of these gatherings are found in institutional churches. If you ever possess the real faith you will be drawn to the most real people who live on this earth. There is a strengthening we all receive when we are joined to others with true faith. But true faith does not worship the temple of God; it worships the God of the temple. When those with the true faith are asked about their faith they do not point to a building or organization, to doctrines or even concepts about truth—they point to the True God.

As the apostle Paul explained, "The kingdom of God does not consist of words, but power." The apostles and prophets foresaw a house of true faith, not being built *by* people but being built *of people*. If you become one of those whose life is being built into that which can contain this power you will easily recognize others who are also a part of the same, not by their creeds or alliances but by the power and the character of the One who has imparted the true faith to them. We must not settle for anything less; good is the worst enemy of best.

It was reported that when Napoleon read the Gospel of John he declared that either Jesus was the Son of God or the one who wrote this gospel was! Napoleon recognized that the genius of true Christianity was far beyond the creative powers of any mere human genius. He then looked at the institution of Christianity and saw no relationship to the Jesus in that gospel. There often is no relationship between the substance of truth and what shallow men try to do with it. Just as it was the most religious and upstanding citizens who crucified Jesus, it is the most religious and upstanding institutions that often destroy true faith in Him.

But true faith will not die in an institution; it is an indestructible power that was able to transform even a few fishermen and humble folk into the greatest force in history, which challenged the greatest empire in history and unraveled it. True faith is a power that could take a few letters written by these simple people and impact history more than all other books combined have been able to do. Just a small portion of this true faith in your life will radically transform you and your destiny.

But we must beware! Only the most courageous have pressed beyond the muddied waters of the pretender faith to taste the pure waters of the true. It was meant to be that way. The power of the true faith is too great to entrust to anyone who will not esteem it as their most precious possession and pay any price to get it. Such is the constitution of all who would rise above mediocrity to the highest place. The wilderness is meant to bring out the best, or the worst, in you; you are the one who decides which it will be.

Paul's exhortation was to "Test yourselves to see if you are in the faith; examine yourselves!" (II Corinthians 13:5) The overemphasis upon *what* we believe instead of *how* we believe has resulted in many becoming more like parrots than like Christ; we can say the right things but our lives are not impacted.

In Acts 1:22 we see that the apostolic office was for the purpose of being *"a witness of His resurrection."* If the message of the resurrection was to be the basis of the apostolic gospel, and the general message that is preached today is producing little true faith in the resurrection, I determined to find out where the departure from this message had begun with the hope of understanding how it could be recovered.

I went through my library searching for the messages on the resurrection by those who are considered some of the greatest men of faith since biblical times. I was astonished at what I found. Of the numerous volumes of teaching and insight from some of these men, they would only have a page or two on the subject of the resurrection! Many of these were obviously just obligatory Easter sermons. How is it that with several centuries of emphasis upon recovering biblical truth that this foundational truth upon which the gospel is based could be so neglected? Is it not time to again recover the meaning and power of the resurrection?

In the biblical church, their belief in the resurrection caused not only faith and power, *but also persecution.*

In my studies it became apparent why this message has been so neglected: in the biblical church, their belief in the resurrection caused not only faith and power *but also persecution.* When Peter and John were dragged before the Sanhedrin it was because the rulers were "being greatly disturbed because they (Peter and John) were teaching the people and proclaiming in Jesus *the resurrection from the dead*" (Acts 4:2). When Paul was later arrested and brought before this same board, he declared, *"I am on trial for the hope and resurrection of the dead!"* Acts 23:6).

There may be little we can do that will bring persecution upon us faster than preaching the message of the resurrection. This is because when we begin to preach this message we are attacking Satan's strongest fortress, his most powerful grip upon this world (including the church)—*the fear of death.* This freedom is a prerequisite to complete freedom in any other area of our lives. The witness of the resurrection had to be the basic message of the apostolic gospel.

Have you ever wondered why more scripture is devoted to Abraham finding a burial place than there is concerning such important subjects as being born again? Why did Isaac and Jacob insist on being buried in the same place? Why would Joseph make Israel swear to carry up his bones to bury him in the same place? And why was that listed in Hebrews chapter eleven as one of the great acts of faith? What difference did it make where they were buried? We see the answer when we read the account of the crucifixion of Jesus in Matthew:

> And Jesus cried out again with a loud voice and yielded up His spirit.
>
> And behold the veil of the temple was torn in two from top to bottom, and the earth shook; and the rocks were split,
>
> and the tombs were opened; *and many of the bodies of the saints who had fallen asleep were raised...*" (Matthew 27:52).

These men had prophetically foreseen the crucifixion and resurrection of Jesus and had positioned themselves to be a part of it. The Lord Himself confirmed this when He said, "Your father Abraham desired to see My day, and he *saw* it and was glad" (John 8:56).

When the "eyes of our hearts" are opened we begin to see the things that are eternal and we are no longer bound by time and by the things which are temporal. Abraham saw with the eyes of His heart. Therefore, he could look ahead to see the crucifixion and resurrection of Jesus and believe in Him just like we do looking back in history.

When we begin to see with the eyes of our hearts instead of just our natural eyes, we do not just begin to see the things that are eternal but they become *more real* to us than the things which are temporary. Then, like Abraham, we do not become overly possessive of anything in the temporary realm. Even the chosen purpose of God in our life, our Isaacs, we will freely give back to God because we know that the resurrection will give them back to us for eternity.

Because Abraham had seen the day of the Lord he understood that Isaac was a "type" (Hebrews 11:19) or prophetic model of the coming Messiah. That is why he made Isaac carry the wood for his own sacrifice just as Jesus was to bear His own cross. That is why he could so confidently say "the Lord will provide for Himself a lamb" (Genesis 22:8). When we have the eyes of our hearts opened to see the purpose and plan of God a faith is imparted to live radically different and free from the bonds of temporal concerns.

But how do we get this faith so that the eyes of our hearts are opened? How do we get our intellectual understanding of biblical truths transferred from our minds to our hearts? The answer to this question is utterly practical: begin to develop a **secret** relationship with God.

Jesus asked His followers, "**How can you believe, when you receive glory from one another, and you do not seek the glory that is from the one and only God**?" (John 5:44). This statement highlighted the fact that one of the most destructive factors undermining true faith is our desire for human recognition. The Lord also warned:

> Beware of practicing your righteousness before men to be noticed by them; *otherwise you have no reward with your Father who is in heaven.*
>
> When therefore you give alms, do not sound a trumpet before you, as the hypocrites do in the synagogues and the streets, that they may be honored by men. Truly I say to you, they have their reward in full.
>
> But when you give alms, do not let your left hand know what your right hand is doing. that your alms may be in secret; and your Father *who sees in secret* will repay you.
>
> And when you pray, you are not to be as the hypocrites; for they love to stand and pray in the synagogues and on the street corners, in order to be seen by men. Truly I say to you, they have their reward in full.
>
> But you, when you pray, go into your inner room, and when you have shut your door, *pray to your Father who is in secret, and your Father who sees in secret will repay you (Matthew 6:1-6).*

Some of the most devoted servants, the most faithful intercessors and the most generous contributors to the Lord's purposes can have little or no reward for their actions in heaven because they have sought mere human recognition for them on earth. When we do this we receive our reward "in full." If we really believed in the resurrection and understood that we are laying up fruit for eternal life, we would not be wasting an eternal inheritance on such trivial and fleeting human recognition and honor.

On the other hand, when we begin to really believe the resurrection in our hearts, we become increasingly focused on laying up fruit for eternal life. We will begin to build that secret relationship with the Father, not wanting anyone but our Father to know about our alms or prayers. When we do this, and our treasure really is being deposited in our "heavenly bank account," where our treasure is there will our heart be also. *When our hearts are with the Father in heaven, the eyes of our hearts start to open and those things which are eternal become more real to us than the things which are passing away.* That is precisely the nature of true faith. ■

---

*Rick Joyner is the founder of MorningStar Publications and the author of several books, including: **There Were Two Trees in the Garden, The Harvest** and his most recent release **Leadership, Management and the Five Essentials For Success**. His prophetic articles "A Vision of the Harvest" and "Onslaught Against the Church" have been widely distributed throughout the body of Christ. Rick also travels throughout the US and abroad as a conference speaker with a message of devotion to Christ and preparation for the coming harvest.*

THE CHURCH AND THE KINGDOM

by Dudley Hall

Through the years of Christian history there has been much discussion and much dissent concerning the Kingdom of God. Whole systems of theological thought have been developed around certain views of the Kingdom. As is true with all doctrine, many well-meaning Christians have naively adopted the view most prominent in their denomination, resulting in misunderstanding or confusion about one of the most important themes of the Bible.

It should not surprise us that there is controversy surrounding this subject; it is too important to be left uncontested by the enemy. When there is controversy concerning a subject, usually the church at large will try to avoid the subject altogether. But can't we do this if we are to walk in the liberty of the Spirit and the truth that sets men free? There will always be a spiritual fight over the "authority" and "power" issues. The truths of healing, deliverance, intercession, spiritual gifts and the kingdom will always be contested, for it is through the proper understanding of these that victory is won and ground is taken by the body of Christ.

The concept of the kingdom of God was the basis for the great hope for Old Testament saints. They looked forward to that time when God's reign would be physically established on the earth. It would be a time of peace and prosperity for God's people as well as all of His creatures. The political situation would be affected by the infusion of real justice into the corrupt political maneuvering of despotic governments. God's economics would bring God's blessings and cause the work of his people to blossom and prosper. They would lend to many but not borrow. The social conditions would be healthy as the poor would receive their supply and the needy helped; there would be righteous handling of the earth's wealth. The religious climate would be heavenly because God would reign on earth dwelling among His people, and all the earth would look to Israel and His Jerusalem for their hope.

In the coming kingdom, people would be at peace, free from bondage, prosperous and healthy. This hope permeated and motivated the Israelites for many generations. It gave them comfort when they were slaves, and courage when they were tempted to despair as the long years seemed to pass them by. There was the ever present unending line of Amorites, Hittites, Jebusites, etc. that could make even the most optimistic saint wonder if victory would ever come. But there was always that promise of the kingdom that kept the ember of hope burning in their souls.

So you can see it was a monumental declaration that day when Jesus the Nazarene stated to these well-informed Israeli theologians, "you must change your way of thinking for the kingdom of God is at hand!" "At hand, what do you mean?" they thought. "If the kingdom is here now what about the political, economic, social & religious changes that we've heard about? Why don't we see the changes?" The kingdom had come in a person—the King, and they would have to be born of the Spirit in order to see this spiritual reality.

Most of those who heard this declaration would not believe it, and they missed seeing what was already in their midst. They watched Jesus heal the sick, raise the dead, cleanse the leper, forgive sin, rebuke demons, but never associated it with the kingdom. They had other explanations for all these phenomena, because they wouldn't believe and couldn't see. They were sure this was not the long hoped for kingdom, not only because it didn't resemble their expectations, but because they were sure they had not yet met the righteous conditions for the kingdom to come. After all, God would not bless sinners; and there were too many of them still around even amongst the Israelites. So they missed the mercy of God while holding tightly to their perception of His holiness.

Sounds a little familiar doesn't it? Many still can't see His kingdom today because they don't believe we have qualified for blessing by being good enough. We've missed the essence of His kingdom. He justifies the sinner! He gives grace to the undeserving and the needy! It requires humility to receive the reality of the kingdom of God, the humility of a little child, and nothing humbles us like receiving what we know you can't earn and would never deserve.

Throughout Jesus' earthly ministry, the kingdom was His theme. He sent His disciples out to preach and practice the kingdom. When He had finished his work on earth, he instructed them to teach others to do what he had taught them. Jesus was not content to preach the kingdom as a new theory, but a reality; therefore he demonstrated it as well as declared it. He healed the sick, demonstrating the superiority of His kingdom to that of Satan's. He cast out demons which obviously revealed His superior authority and power over them. He forgave sinners, raised the dead, spoke to the raging sea and in every encounter with every earthly or demonic kingdom, He revealed superiority.

Some are anxiously quick to point out that he did not heal all the sick, raise all the dead, etc, and conclude that this proves the kingdom had not come. I think it would be more accurate to say the kingdom had come but will not be consummated until the end of the age. The deposit is here now, and the fulfillment will be realized when Jesus returns to the earth in bodily form. We receive some things now and some we get then. For instance, we have healing now and glorified bodies then. We have forgiveness of sins now and perfection then; we have victory over the enemy now, annihilation of the enemy then. So there is the reality of the kingdom *now* and the reality of the kingdom *then*. We must not delay the "now" until the "then," or try to force the "then" to happen "now."

Those who postpone the kingdom totally are forced to live in an interim of exasperated unfulfillment and confused motivation. According to some who have this view, the kingdom is not going to come until Jesus gets back, and He isn't coming back until things get so bad the church will have to be snatched out in order to exist at all. If this is true why should we be a part of preventing society from corruption and destruction? The faster things get worse, the sooner He'll return and get the original plan back into operation. The world is evil and corrupt and we are here to snatch as many souls into a temporary "foxhole" as we can. Don't get involved with filthy endeavors such as political, economic, social issues, public education, etc. These are worldly and belong to the spiritually dead world. "Let the dead bury the dead" we hear quoted, "we must just win souls."

But win them to what? To be saved from eternal punishment is wonderful, but is that all there is to salvation? Are they to be left in their salvation "foxhole" simply to wait and warn everybody else to get into the "foxhole" with them? Sounds like a lower purpose for life than the eternal abundant life that Jesus talked about. Paul's "ruling and reigning in life" (Romans 5:17) sounds a little more exciting that the fearful refugee mentality of those who are "occupying" until the kingdom comes. What kind of hope and confidence can the church have when it is convinced that authority and

In the absence of kingdom structure we've adopted the business world's corporate structure.

power have been suspended? The church is not just a parenthesis in God's plan until He can get back to natural Israel. The church is called to be the light of the world, the salt of this earth, and you cannot be either with a foxhole mentality. Jesus did not leave healing in the hands of medical science, deliverance to the psychologist, and social change to the corrupt world system. He left all of them in the hands of His church!

To those who would object that saving the lost is our only objective, I object! Jesus said, "Going into all the world, **make disciples**, baptizing them...and teaching them to do what I have taught you." What did He teach them to do (not just to know)? To proclaim the Kingdom of God and reveal its presence by healing the sick, casting out demons, cleansing the leper, etc. We are to save the lost! YES! But we are to save them to a full life of grace and glory now as well as hope for the fulfillment of the kingdom. They are saved to live in the reality of His invisible kingdom being made visible through people who live by its realities.

Through the years there has been much confusion because people have identified the church as the kingdom and the kingdom as the church. It is interesting to note that in the New Testament they are never equated. Jesus never taught us to preach the church. It was never intended to be the subject of our preaching or proclamation. Throughout the New Testament we are continually exhorted to proclaim and practice the realities of the kingdom. This is what the apostles did throughout the book of Acts, and it is to be included in the acts of the church until this age does come to a close. One of the last statements made concerning the ministry of Paul is in Acts 28:30 "And he stayed two full years in his own rented quarters welcoming all who came to him, *preaching the kingdom of God* and teaching concerning the Lord Jesus Christ with all openness unhindered." This too is what the church will be found doing until the end, preaching the kingdom and teaching about Jesus *with all openness!*

Some have argued that the kingdom is not mentioned very much in the Epistles as evidence that the kingdom has been suspended until a later time, thus validating the theory that the church is a parenthesis in the overall plan of God. A more accurate and appropriate interpretation would be that the church is seen as an agent of the kingdom being the visible expression of the invisible reality which is the kingdom itself.

Focusing on the church as the message has only resulted in confusion and endless divisions. First of all it produces disillusionment because the church is a living organism which will continue to flux and change in its process toward maturity; it has not yet fully become what it is called to become. Therefore, the church will always be incomplete and imperfect until Jesus' return. When we preach the church people are easily repelled because they see her many imperfections. The kingdom on the other hand is the rule of God and can be confidently proclaimed in any culture and in any generation because the rule of God is never imperfect.

Secondly, those who proclaim the church as their central message end up with a mentality of self preservation and competition. We try to protect our reason for existence as a local church and become competitive toward all of those who are trying to get people to fill their churches. This translates into sectarianism and a provincialism preventing the unity of the body. It is the unity of the church that was the essence of Jesus' prayer for His people in John 17 and is the essence of its witness to the world. When our minds get so focused upon our own local assembly that we neither have time nor vision to include the other churches in our area or their world, we have failed to discern the Lord's body properly. Even in the first century church Paul declared that this was the primary reason for the weakness, sickness and death in the church.

It seems that every local church on almost every corner feels that it is their responsibility to meet every need of the community. This is a subtle way of saying that no other church in the community is needed because "we will handle all the problems." This also promotes the belief that if anyone attends another church it must be because they are less spiritual or are not as committed as we are. The fact is God has placed His many faceted body over all the earth and not every local church is to meet every need of the community. Some churches will be called on to focus on one area of need while others will focus on something totally different. When we begin to cooperate together, and to love and support one another, the church really will become the "light of the world," providing the answer to the world's problems and darkness. It is only those who have a kingdom mentality who are able to relate on such a basis. Their allegiance is to the kingdom of God not just to a local assembly. They are committed to God *through* their local assembly. This is not to become a "floating charismatic," but to have an overview of the purpose of God rising above our little parochial visions of the present. As the invisible kingdom of God is expressed through the visible agent of the church, the world begins to see that there is some higher form of living possible and thus anyone in the world can become a candidate for the grace of God.

Kingdom Structure

One of the significant failures of the visible church has been its adoption of the world's structure for its organization. In the absence of kingdom structure we've adopted the business world's corporate structure. We have pastors who act as C.E.O.'s and deacons and elders who act as the Board of Directors. The rest of the people become the resources for money and ideas to carry out the goals of producing a good organization. Our success is too often measured by how many people we can get involved in our programs and filling our buildings, or even just how well organized we are. The problem is that we can get a lot of people motivated but they just don't go anywhere or really do anything.

In the kingdom we find Jesus, who is the King of the kingdom, being the actual Head of His body, the church. That means He is the One making the decisions and conveying them to those He has chosen to be the spiritual leaders of the church. The leaders He has chosen can be seen as the neck of the body whose purpose is simply to convey the message of the Head down to the body so that the body operates in unity and accomplishes the goals that the Head has set forth. If we are really connected to the Head, we will get the same results Jesus did with His ministry: the sick will be healed, the captives set free, we will have access to God's provision for the present yet our focus will turn from the temporary to the eternal kingdom. Such is the primary purpose of the manifestations of the kingdom which accompany the preaching of the kingdom.

When Jesus heard His disciples discussing who would be the greatest in the kingdom His answer to them was something like this: In the world of the Gentiles you lord it over one another but in the kingdom of God it will not be so. He who is servant of all will be greatest of all. In that wonderful declaration Jesus gave the kingdom of God's principle of structure. It can be defined in two words—"mutual submission".

Mutual submission means that every person in the body of Christ gets to submit to every other person at some time or another. Since Jesus is the Head He gets to do the choosing and the directing. He picks by giving gifts to people and anointing them. Our responsibility is to simply recognize His gifts and anointings. How does Jesus appoint the leaders? By giving them leadership abilities. It is essential that a man who is called to be an elder or an overseer has the ability to oversee.

God gives gifts and anointings and we simply recognize His choice and submit to the one who has that gift. When someone is gifted with prophecy we submit to that gift; when one is gifted in teaching we submit to that gift; when one is gifted in the ability to oversee we submit to that gift; when one is gifted to exhort we submit to that gift, etc. So we all end up submitting to others who have different gifts and callings than ourselves. God has designed the body to work this way so that interdependence would be necessary. Everybody has a place and must depend upon others in order for the body to be healthy. With this approach everybody has a sense of significance and importance. No one is seen as a second rate citizen, and no one feels the unnecessary burden of having to be a leader alone. There is only One Head and that is Jesus; there is no competition for His part. All the rest of us are operating in our gifts, under our anointings, submitting to each other.

Man left alone to choose his leadership will always seem to choose one man. As Israel chose Saul to be their king, we will look for one man and place all of the responsibility upon his shoulders and create out of our expectations a role model for him that is impossible to fulfill. A modern day evangelical pastor has an impossible role. If he succeeds with God he will fail by the expectations of man; if he succeeds in fulfilling the expectations of man he will almost

continued on page 45

Elijah and the End Times

by Aaron Katz

The following is a condensed excerpt from the book *REALITY: The Hope Of Glory*, published and distributed by MorningStar Publications.

As the Lord God of Israel Liveth, Before Whom I Stand...

We hear nothing about this great man of God, Elijah, before his abrupt introduction at the very beginning of all seventeenth chapter of 1 Kings. We see him there, in all the fulness and power of the Holy Spirit, standing before Ahab with complete fearlessness, speaking words of awesome intensity:

> "And Elijah the Tishbite, who was of the inhabitants of Gilead, said unto Ahab, As the Lord God of Israel liveth, before whom I stand, there shall not be dew nor rain these years, but according to my word." 1 Kings 17:1

This verse is like the blowing of a trumpet. It is the presentation of an unheard of man onto the stage of history in a perfect moment in the timing of God. I love God's discretion; it does not please Him to raise the curtain and let us see what it took to prepare and shape such a vessel as Elijah. There is only silence and obscurity.

We can safely assume that the spiritual mountain peak on which this prophet stood could have only been preceded by the "pit" of God's dealing. For men like Joseph and Elijah, submitted in their hearts to the will of God, each pit is a school of the Spirit, where, progressively and gradually, every confidence in the flesh is exposed and cut away. Before our Lord brings His disciples before the Pharaohs and Ahabs in this world, there must always be a period of crucial preparation in osbcurity.

This pattern is true even of our Lord Himself. Except for a few incidents surrounding His birth and one youthful episode in the temple of Jerusalem, we know not a thing about the first thirty years of His life. Obscurity. Maybe that's where our life is now, individually and corporately, as the Body of Christ. Unseen and in places unknown to others, the Lord is dealing with us and bringing us low—into pits.

"There shall not be dew nor rain these years, but according to my word." What manner of man is this who presumes to command the elements? This would be an act of unspeakable gall, arrogance of embarrassing proportions, if Elijah was not so wholly hidden in God. In effect, it was not even he who was speaking, but the God Who possessed his life. In the yoke of loving obedience, God and His servant could work together in perfect unity, for "...he that is joined unto the Lord is one spirit (1 Corinthians 6:17). It is to this place of intimate union with Him that the Lord is bringing those who are *willing* in the present hour, and the shaping of such vessels is not accomplished in one day.

Elijah was not afraid that he might be accused of infringing upon God or of attempting to steal His glory. He spoke boldly, for he knew that the two halves of his statement are perfectly related. There is no way that a man can command the elements without first affirming "As the Lord God of Israel liveth, before whom I stand."

To stand before the Living God means being closed in with Him while being separated from the world. Yet, this is only part of the implication, the easier part; the more fearful and demanding aspect entails separation not only from the world but sometimes even from your own brethren in the faith. Many of us have graduated from worrying about what the world says of us. Have we, however, come to a place of such maturity that we can live with the scorn of our brothers? That is not an easy place to come to, because we have perhaps just begun to really enjoy the prestige and acceptance of men, in this case, *Christian* men. The man who can stand before the King Ahabs of this world has got to be that one who stands before God continually. He must ultimately be indifferent to the opinions of both the world and those who call themselves by the Lord's name.

I am neither encouraging you to rebellion nor to looking askance upon the elders whom God has placed over you. In fact, I am deeply committed to the principle of submission to authority, and to all the principles of relationship within the Body of Christ which are clearly delineated in the Scriptures. Yet, in the same breath, I must stress that there is required of every child of God an independence of the spirit and a tenacious cleaving and fidelity to the Lord, even when a situation might arise where it is seemingly impossible to give those closest to you an acceptable explanation.

The Way of Obscurity

The magnitude of Elijah's act of speaking his strong words to Ahab can be appreciated all the more when we consider the character of that king. We read that:

> "...Ahab the son of Omri *did evil in the sight of the Lord above all that were before him.*
>
> And it came to pass, as if it had been a light thing for him *to walk in the sins of Jereboam* the son of Nebat, that he took to wife Jezebel the daughter of Ethbaal king of the Zidonians, and went and served Baal, and worshipped him.
>
> And he reared up an altar for Baal in the house of Baal, which he had built in Samaria.
>
> And Ahab made a grove; *and Ahab did more to provoke the Lord God of Israel to anger than all the kings of Israel that were before him.*" 1 Kings 16:30-33 (our italics)

The abundance of evil that existed in the reign of Obscurity became a standard of darkness by which the apostasy of each succeeding ruler was measured. Nadab, Baasha, Elah, Zimri, Omri: each of these kings walked in that way, and with each one the extremity of Israel's departure from holiness was increased. Of all these black-hearted despots, Ahab was the worst. His wife Jezebel had singlehandedly seen to the execution of most of God's prophets. Elijah was the only one left. It is before *that* man that he stood, making with resolute calm and boldness, that statement which is illustrative of his entire ministry.

> "And he made an house of high places, made priests of the lowest of the people, which were not of the sons of Levi." I Kings 12:31

My guess is that Obscurity may have established a few seminaries, passed men through their career courses, and given them pulpits. These men were not of the Levites; *they were not God's appointed messengers.* In short, their ministries were not born in heaven.

There are countless functionaries and religious practitioners running rampant in this age. There is a world dying because of the false equation of that self-ordained group with the representatives of the Most High God. We have not yet seen the end of the ways of Obscurity.

There is a world church that is going to be formed that will preach a religion of convenience. In it, you shall not have to sweat to go up to Jerusalem; everything shall be easily accessible, and nothing shall be required of you. Dropping a dollar in the collection plate will suffice to ease the whimperings of conscience. The men who shall minister in its temples shall perhaps speak the conventional terminology, but *they shall not know God.* Such men are not "Levites," not God's priests. There is but one true priesthood; it is comprised of all those who have been born again of the Spirit, and who are wholly cleaving to the Living God:

> "But ye are a chosen generation, *a royal priesthood,* an holy nation, a peculiar people; that ye should shew forth the praises of him who hath called you out of darkness into his marvelous light:
>
> Which in time past were not a people, but are now the people of God: which had not obtained mercy, but now have obtained mercy." I Peter 2:9,10 (our italics)

The false priesthood of this world shall enmesh itself in a particular type of worship. It is nothing new.

> "And Jeroboam ordained a feast in the eighth month, on the fifteenth day of the month, *like unto the feast that is in Judah,* and he offered upon the altar. So did he in Bethel, sacrificing unto the calves that he had made: and he placed in Bethel the priests of the high places which he had made." I Kings 12:32 (our italics)

That feast was counterfeit; it appeared to be, but it was not, the real thing ordained of God in His time.

The configuration of false gods, false priests, and false worship is a perfect picture of the "church" which is going to be raised up in the end times. The foundation of that structure has already been laid.

The world at the end of the tenth century, B.C. had never seen a fuller expression of the way of Obscurity than in the reign of Ahab. In his marriage to Jezebel we witness the union of politics and religion. The Zidonians practiced a form of religion which had idolatry and orgiastic self-indulgence at the heart of it. It is before a configuration such as this that God is going to bring a people who will stand like Elijah, and speak the word of the Lord.

The Voice of the Master

> "And the word of the Lord came unto him, saying,
>
> Get thee hence, and turn thee eastward, and hide thyself by the brook Cherith, that is before Jordan.
>
> And it shall be, that thou shalt drink of the brook; and I have commanded the ravens to feed thee there." I Kings 17:2-4

Had not Elijah been so joined to the Lord, he might have thought, upon receiving this word, "Uh oh, that's not God's voice. I'm wise to wiles of the enemy; I know what he's up to. That devil just wants to get me out of the wilderness and divert me from my appointed task. And ravens! Why, that's the last kind of instrumentality an all-wise God would use to feed His prophet. They're birds of prey, scavengers, garbage eaters. This is obviously just a satanic attempt to destroy me." But we read at the beginning of the next verse: "So he went and did according unto the word of the Lord" (verse 5a).

How did Elijah know that he was hearing the voice of the Lord? He knew in the only way that any of us can: he was familiar with the accents, the tone, the character of his God. That familiarity and knowledge is not born in a day, but is the result of repeated hearings and repeated acts of obedience.

Getting to know the Lord's voice is inextricably linked to understanding His *way.* Why would God choose ravens to feed a prophet? How foolish and illogical. Yet God will choose those things which are foolish in the world's estimation to confound the worldly-wise (see 1 Corinthians

1:18-31).

I would have been suspicious if the voice which Elijah heard had said, "There shall be a Jewish caterer to sustain thee with three square meals a day, a nosh before bedtime, and the best gefilte fish this side of the Jordan." When I heard "ravens," I thought, "Ah, that's my God."

He is a God Who chose, when He penetrated time-space history in bodily form, to be born in a stable. Almost all of the Jews of that generation rejected their King. They knew neither the voice of God nor His distinctive way. There is nothing more necessary for the people of God of our generation than the appropriation of that knowledge which comes as a consequence of walking with the Author of grace day after day and year after year.

Kneeling at the Dried Brook

> "So he went and did according unto the word of the Lord: for he went and dwelt by the brook Cherith, that is before Jordan.
>
> And the ravens brought him bread and flesh in the morning, and bread and flesh in the evening; and he drank of the brook.
>
> And it came to pass after a while, that *the brook dried up*, because there had been no rain in the land." I Kings 17:5-7 (italics ours)

What kind of God is this, anyway? He brings the prophet to a brook, a place of security, well-being, and provision, and then allows that brook to dry up! In the years that I have walked with my Lord, He has repeatedly shown me that this is His characteristic way.

The lesson is simple: don't look down to "brooks"—*look up to the Father of lights*. Looking down was the hang-up of the Chaldeans. Ur of the Chaldees, birthplace of Abram, was situated on the banks of the Euphrates River. The natives of that place were utterly dependent upon that body of water for their commerce and culture—indeed, for their life itself! God called Abram away from that visible source. He no longer looked down to that river. God's friend raised his eyes upward to the promise of a land of early and latter rains.

God is preparing us *now* for total dependence on Him, and is weaning us from every kind of thing in which we have found a false security. Every brook that we have worshiped and consider to be the *source* of our nourishment shall be, by our God's merciful hand, utterly dried up.

So He Arose and Went

> "And the word of the Lord came unto him (Elijah), saying,
>
> Arise, get thee to Zarephath, which belongeth to Zidon, and dwell there: behold, I have commanded a widow woman there to sustain thee." I Kings 17:8,9

How would the natural mind, still hankering after that Jewish caterer, respond to this command? "Oh, come on, Lord. Listen to reason. This is not even a Jewish woman you're sending me to. It was bad enough with that raven business, but Zidon is where Jezebel herself comes from. Those heathen know no limits to their wickedness, and right now they are suffering in the famine that I myself proclaimed. Now, really Lord, is that Zidonian woman going to sustain a Hebrew prophet? Never happen!"

The Scripture says of Elijah, "so he arose and went to Zarephath" (verse 10a). As many times as I read those words, great delight springs up in my soul. Sometimes, I say to people, half jokingly, "If you have something to do with my burial and you want to put a nice inscription on my tombstone besides, 'Arthur Katz, date of birth, date deceased,' one quotation will do beautifully: 'So he arose and went,' or, perhaps, 'So he went and did according unto the word of the Lord.'" My prayer is that such a statement may be, in the final analysis, a true description of my time on this earth.

So he arose and went, no ifs, no ands, no buts, no maybes, no arguing with God, no scratching his head and reviewing all the good, logical reasons why God's commandment could not possibly be fulfilled. Such a man is not fashioned in a day, and the shaping process is not necessarily pleasant. Every one of us has a craven heart, itching for a facile security, and reluctant to be separated from the egotistical hang-ups and fleshly cravings upon which we have built our lives.

Without spiritual heart surgery by the hand of God, there can be no standing before Ahab, and no life of sustained yieldingness to our Lord's bidding. Cutting away is never painless, but when God holds the scalpel the motive is clear, and the victory is sure:

"And the Lord thy God will circumcise thine heart, and the heart of thy seed, to love the Lord thy God with all thine heart, and with all thy soul, that thou mayest live." Deuteronomy 30:6

See, Thy Son Liveth

"So he arose and went to Zarephath. And when he came to the gate of the city, behold, the widow woman was there gathering of sticks: and he called to her, and said, Fetch me, I pray thee, a little water in a vessel, that I may drink.

And as she was going to fetch it, he called to her, and said, Bring me, I pray thee, a morsel of bread in thine hand.

And she said, As the Lord thy God liveth, I have not a cake, but an handful of meal in a barrel, and a little oil in a cruse: and, behold, I am gathering two sticks, that I may go in and dress it for me and my son, that we may eat it, and die."
I Kings 17:10-12

We see here a woman who is dying of much more than physical starvation. This is a picture of a person who is disconsolate, broken, disillusioned, and depressed. There is the suggestion of one who had lived "high on the hog," one who had enjoyed affluence, comfort, and luxury, and who had, all of a sudden, had the bottom pulled out from under her. That widow is a good representation of the world to which God shall send us in an Elijah type ministry at the end of the ages.

After the crash of 1929, men and women committed suicide in record numbers. We can expect to see a repeat performance of this kind of response when economic catastrophe strikes again. Our generation has not been fitted to hold up under conditions of famine. Dispirited, it shall be ready to eat its last meal, roll over, and die.

"And Elijah said unto her, Fear not, go and do as thou hast said: but make me thereof a little cake first, and bring it unto me, and after make for thee and for my son.

For thus saith the Lord God of Israel, "The barrel of meal shall not waste, neither shall the cruse of oil fail, until the day the Lord sendeth rain upon the earth."

And she went and did according to the saying of Elijah: and she, and he, and her house, did eat many days.

And the barrel of meal wasted not, neither did the cruse of oil fail, according to the word of the Lord, which he spake by Elijah." I Kings 17:13-16

This miraculous provision, confirming the truth of the prophetic word spoken by Elijah, was still not enough to effect the salvation of the widow woman. She may have been grateful to the prophet, and perhaps even to God, for the physical sustenance, but, spiritually, there was no regeneration.

"And it came to pass after these things, that the son of a woman, the mistress of the house, fell sick; and his sickness was so sore, that there was no breath left in him." I Kings 17:17

Nothing less than the death of her son could have brought that Zidonian widow woman to the necessary brokenness that precedes real contrition. She had nothing left that mattered to her but one son, and he was more dear to her than her own life. When God took her son's life, the stone walls of that mother's heart were smashed and the light of the Spirit shone in:

> "And she said unto Elijah, What have I to do with thee, O thou man of God? *Art thou come unto me to call my sin to remembrance, and to slay my son?* I Kings 17:18 (our italics)

This woman was certainly no great scholar, but somehow she understood that the abrupt taking of her son was directly and intimately related to her own spiritual condition before God. "Art thou come unto me to call *my* sin to remembrance." Would to God that the more tutored people might equally understand that the dealings we receive at His hand have to do with unconfessed sin and a consequent separation from a loving Father.

> "Or despisest thou the riches of his goodness and forbearance and longsuffering; not knowing that *the goodness of God leadeth to repentance?* Romans 2:4 (our italics)

Many may inquire, "Is it *good* to take a woman's only son?" The answer must be "*Yes*,if it will save a soul from eternal burning." Wherever people are vulnerable, *there* will God touch them. If a man is indifferent about his own life and is ready to go to hell, then God may put His finger on the person or thing which is more precious than himself. The Lord is "...not willing that any should perish, but that all should come to repentance" (2 Peter 3:9b).

Like Joseph on many occasions before him, this prophet found himself surprised by a critical situation of which he had neither forewarning nor explanation from God. Again, crisis revealed the true mettle of a man. The same touchstone shall be used increasingly at the end of the ages. Elijah, joined to the Lord and one spirit with Him, acted instantly:

> "And he said unto her, Give me thy son. And he took him out of her bosom, and carried him up into a loft, where he abode, and laid him upon his own bed.
>
> And he cried unto the Lord, and said, O Lord my God, hast thou also brought evil upon the widow and whom I sojourn, by slaying her son?
>
> And he stretched himself upon the child three times, and cried unto the Lord, and said, O Lord my God, I pray thee, let this child's soul come into him again.
>
> "And the Lord heard the voice of Elijah; and the soul of the child came into him again, and he revived." I Kings 17:19-22

We see here *not* simply an interesting historical narrative of one man's reaction to an unexpected and untoward circumstance; in Elijah's response, God is showing us *today* the definitive pattern of His end-time evangelism. He is calling us to the corpse of a dead world. We have hoped that we could save it with bumper stickers, literature campaigns, "Christian" pop music, and countless other human programs, all without a modicum of embarrassment. "No stoop, no fuss, no bother."

This world shall be saved only by the willingness of men and women to take the stiff, cold, wretched cadaver of the world up to their abode, *where their own bed is*, and stretch it out on their satiny smooth sheets. "Oh, Art, listen, I was willing to come to the conferences and the potluck dinners, but my bed is my own private domain." EXACTLY. There is no shortcut: if we are not willing to have that privacy penetrated by a holy burden and concern for the world, we shall play no active part in its revival.

Stretched out upon that corpse, fingertip to fingertip, eyeball to eyeball, and jowl to jowl, the prophet cried to the Lord three times, "Let breath come back to this dead child." Elijah, seen and heard only by God, was moving in the same Spirit as Moses, when he interceded for a spiritually dead Israel:

> "Yet now, if thou wilt forgive their sin—; and if not, blot me, I pray thee, out of thy book which thou hast written." Exodus 32:32

It is the same attitude that Paul expressed as he spoke from his heart about his Jewish people:

> "For I could wish that myself were accursed from Christ for my brethren, my kinsmen according to the flesh.
>
> Who are Israelites; to whom pertaineth the adoption, and the glory, and the covenants, and the giving of the law, and the service of God, and the promises;
>
> Whose are the fathers, and of whom as concerning the flesh Christ came, who is over all, God blessed for ever. Amen. Romans 9:3-5

David's son Absalom was slain while attempting to overthrow his father's kingdom. When the king heard of the death, he did not rejoice over the death of an enemy:

> "And the king was much moved, and went up to the chamber over the gate, and as he went, thus he said, O my son Absalom, my son, my son Absalom! Would to God that I had died for thee, O Absalom, my son, my son!" II Samuel 18:33

In all of these lives, we see the love of Christ shed abroad in men's hearts by the Holy Spirit. From the mouth of Elijah God heard the cries of a man after His own heart. In that moment, that prophet's whole body, pressed against the dead boy, became a living prayer: "O Lord my God, take the breath which is in me, take the *life* which is in me, and put it within this child."

The spirit of the world has permeated and corrupted the attitudes of the Body of Christ. We have taken upon ourselves business mentalities, and have thought that, through devices, stratagems, and programs, we could save a world. There can never be life without, first, a willingness to suffer death. It is the cardinal principle of God, and is inseparable from the central meaning of His cross. "So then death worketh in us," Paul said, "but life in you" (II Corinthians 4:12). There has got to be a readiness to prostrate ourselves out over a dead world—in all of its clammy cold stiffness—and, as our sheets get soiled, cry out of the kishkes, out of the gut, three times or three hundred times, "Lord, let him live!"

> "And Elijah took the child, and brought him down out of the chamber into the house, and delivered him unto his mother: and Elijah said, *See, thy son liveth."* 1 Kings 17:23 (our italics)

Shall anything less suffice? The world has heard all of our slogans, our clever little sayings, and it is still unmoved. It shall take more than words to pierce through the rigid walls of their hearts; they are longing unknowingly for a demonstration of the resurrection life of God. "For the kingdom of God is not in work, but in power" (1 Corinthians 4:20).

The Word in Thy Mouth

> And the woman said to Elijah, "Now by this I know that thou art a man of God, and that the word of the Lord in thy mouth is truth." II Kings 17:24

"That other stuff was impressive. I really enjoyed the barrel of meal not wasting and the cruse of oil not failing; but now by *this*, life where there was death in my dear son, I know that you are God's man, and in *your* mouth His word is truth." I used to believe that the word of God in our mouths is *always* truth. How can we believe that if we parrot the correct words we are somehow expressing the truth of the Lord? In many of our mouths, these pronouncements amount to hardly more than a religious belch.

As a young believer, there was a phenomenon that would really baffle me. I could hear a certain message preached ten times (how many new messages are there?), and nine times out of ten I would be left completely unimpressed. I would leave the room, the words already forgotten, and my thoughts would cluster around such issues as, "Where am I gonna eat?" Then the tenth man would arrive and

continued on page 44

DISCOVERING YOUR DESTINY

How To Know God's Will For Your Life

by Floyd McClung Jr.
with Geoff and Janet Benge

There are times when each of us asks the question: What is my destiny? We all want to know what God has in store for us in the future. We puzzle as to whether it takes years of clever detective work to discover God's will, or if it's plain and easy to find. This question affects whom we will marry, our profession, where we live, and how we respond to unfolding opportunities for ministry.

In a world of so many choices, it's not always easy to know in which direction we should be heading as Christians. Opportunities seem to abound. There are many open doors in front of us, and even a few tantalizing closed doors! More than ever we need to know that God is leading us in the decisions we make and the direction we take in life.

The principles I am presenting are not just theories, they have been tested many times over in my own experience and in the lives of those I live and work with. They are principles that can be put into practice right now to help you discover the destiny God has in store for your life.

I am a firm believer in divine guidance. The Bible teaches that God cares about the choices we make in life and that He has specific plans for us in every important choice we make. We can learn to hear God's voice, though it is not always easy. God's plans for us begin with His purposes for all mankind (Ephesians 1:11), and extend to the specific purposes He has for us as individuals (Isaiah 46:11; Psalm 40:5; Acts 16:6). Bible writers often speak of doing God's will, both in reference to obedience to God's precepts and principles, and also in relationship to specific obedience to something God wants us to do for Him (Psalm 40:8; Romans 12:1-2; 2 Corinthians 1:17; Romans 15:28, 29; Acts 13:2,4; 2 Samuel 5:19).

God is committed to guiding us far more than we realize. He wants to teach us many lessons about His character and His ways. Psalm 32:8 says He is watching over us to ensure that we miss none of His blessing and plans for us. He wants us to do His will more than we do!

Have you ever looked at a city skyline and marvelled at the buildings? Walls of reflective glass and massive concrete pillars looming ever upwards — colorful mosaics balanced against the sky. Seldom do we pause to wonder that for every towering office building there is a rigid frame of steel and cement holding it in place. The frame may be hidden from immediate view by all the glistening glass but, nevertheless, it is there, and if it were not the building would become a pile of shattered window panes and rubble.

So it is with guidance. Specific guidance is like the glass on a skyscraper — it is necessary but cannot support itself; it must have a structure beneath it. For the Christian, that support structure is made up of godly character and obedience to the revealed truth of God's Word. There are many things in life we don't need to pray about — we need to understand and obey. Most of God's will for our life is already revealed in the Bible.

Scripture reveals certain principles and truths that are God's will for us regardless of our personal situations and circumstances. Obedience to God in these areas is the prerequisite for knowing more of His will. To know God's will for the future, we must obey what we already know in the present!

As we look more closely at what God's Word says about His plan and purposes for our lives, let me suggest that you take a notebook and write the verse for each area at the top of a page. Prayerfully ask God to show you whether you are at present fulfilling His will in this area of your life. Refer back to your notebook on a regular basis and ask, 'Am I closer to God in this area now than I was six months ago?'

❒ It is God's will that we believe in the Lord Jesus.

And this is His commandment, that we believe in the name of His Son Jesus Christ... (1 John 3:23)

Belief in God and faith in His Son Jesus Christ is the most fundamental truth of the Bible, and without it we can never be Christians. Indeed, Christians in the early church were known as 'believers'. They heard of the things Jesus said and did, they read the letters the apostles and other eye witnesses wrote, and they believed.

The Philippian jailer asked, 'What must I do to be saved?' Paul's answer was refreshingly simple, 'Believe in the Lord Jesus and you shall be saved' (Acts 16:30-31). We must never forget that belief in the Lord Jesus is the cornerstone of our Christian faith and is therefore God's will for our lives. He wants a relationship with each one of us, and that is why He sent His Son into the world.

❒ It is God's will that we give ourselves 100% to Him.

I urge you therefore, brethren, by the mercies of God, to present your bodies a living and holy sacrifice, acceptable to God, which is your spiritual service of worship (Romans 12:1).

Many people want to know God's will to decide whether or not they will obey it! They have the attitude of 'Give me plenty of warning God. Tell me both sides of the story, and I'll decide and get in touch with you if I'm available.' God, however, expects unconditional surrender from us. The fact that Almighty God asks for our surrender should be enough to totally guarantee it! We are not two equals locked in debate; only pride can fool us into that delusion. We are finite, God is infinite. We are fallible, He is infallible. We waver, He is constant. We are the created, He is the creator. He is without fault and we are sinners, and He asks us to submit ourselves to His will because of who He is. He is the only wise God and He knows what is best for us in every situation of life.

God's purposes for mankind are always benevolent and merciful. He is for us, not against us (Romans 8:28-32). He longs to save and redeem people, and wants to see each of us reach our full potential. Because of His wonderful character, we can trust Him and have complete confidence in His character and His purpose for our lives.

God wants one hundred per cent of our life, not given out of fear, but out of love and gratitude for who He is and what He has done on the cross. Christianity is not something we can ease into gradually. It is not a democracy where we give fifty-one per cent today, ten per cent next year, and so on until we have finally given ourself one hundred per cent to Him. If we dictate to God how much of our lives He can have then we have not surrendered at all. Instead, we have retained lordship of our lives, and, even if we yield ninety-nine per cent of our lives to Him, we are still in control. Giving our lives 100% to the Lord does not mean we are perfect, it just means we are surrendered! What God wants to hear from us in, 'Anything, anytime, anywhere. I trust you Lord. You speak and I will obey.'

❒ It is God's will that we love the lost.

The Lord is not slow about His promise, as some count slowness, but is patient toward you, not wishing for any to perish, but for all to come to repentance (II Peter 3:9).

God yearns for people to hear the Gospel and be saved. What are we doing to see His will fulfilled in this area? Sharing the gospel is not the responsibility of a handful of 'professional' Christians, it is the responsibility of all Christians.

There are those Christians who have no difficulty sharing the gospel. They have an outgoing personality that enables them to preach on street corners, pray at their office desk, or pass out tracts to strangers in the subway. Many of us, however, are not that bold, yet we still have a responsibility to share His love with others.

God made each of us the way we are. He gave us our personality and we must find ways to share the gospel that are consistent with our personality. We may never stand and preach on a street corner, but we could pray for the person who does. We may be uncomfortable handing out tracts, but we could volunteer to fold those tracts for the person who hands them out. In fact, we may never have anything to do with tracts and street meetings. God may want us to share the gospel with business associates. We could share a Christian record or magazine with a friend, or we could try to meet a specific need we know they have. There are hundreds of creative and effective ways to share the gospel and we must allow God to show us ways that are effective for us. Each of us needs to pray and ask God for opportunities to do His will in the area of evangelism. Don't be deterred. You can, and must make a difference!

❒ It is God's will that we do good works in Christ.

We are His workmanship, created in Christ Jesus for good works, which God prepared beforehand, that we should walk in them (Ephesians 2:10).

James tells us faith without works is dead. Faith is the inward part of our Christian life, the part no one can see. Good works, on the other hand, are the outward part. Everyone can see our good works, or lack of them, but they cannot see the state of our faith.

Faith is like the roots of a tree, and works are the fruit. We don't judge how healthy a tree is by digging it up and inspecting its roots. Instead, we examine its fruit. If there is no fruit, we assume the roots to be diseased or dying. Likewise, if there are no good works visible in our lives as Christians, then our faith is in bad shape. If this is the case it is imperative we examine our faith and correct this problem lest our faith die altogether. Are we doing good works in the situation God as placed us in? They don't need to be spectacular, they can be simple things like babysitting a friend's children, or helping a neighbor get his car started on a cold morning. Seek out opportunities to serve others. Do good works in Jesus' name. If the prospect of doing good works doesn't excite you then you need to expose your roots of faith to the Holy Spirit and have Him tend them.

❒ It is God's will that we grow spiritually.

Make every effort to supplement your faith with virtue, and virtue with knowledge, and knowledge with self-control, and self-control with steadfastness, and steadfastness with godliness, and godliness with brotherly affection, and brotherly affection with love (II Peter 1:5-7 RSV).

Some extremes in theological thinking suggest we ask the Lord into our lives and then sit back and wait for Him to take us to heaven. These verses certainly do not confirm that view. We are to make every effort to increase our faith, our knowledge, our self-control, our steadfastness, and our brotherly affection. Each of us is expected to take responsibility for our spiritual growth, be spiritually self-sustaining. We cannot rely on pastors or Christian leaders to keep our faith propped up. Some Christians live from Sunday to Sunday. They start their week ready for action, but by Saturday are drained of their enthusiasm and can barely drag themselves to church the next day for another boost. While this is not altogether unexpected in a new Christian, if it persists something is seriously amiss.

Paul talks of digesting the 'milk of the word', as compared to the 'meat of the world'. A baby needs someone to feed it milk, and in the same way, a new Christian needs someone to help them understand Biblical truth. We have all seen retarded adults who are incapable of feeding themselves. Behavior that is natural and cute in an infant is pitiful and saddening to watch in these adults. Sadly, there are Christians who are the same spiritually because they have not made 'every effort to supplement their faith'.

Prayer and Bible study are important in supplementing our faith. God reveals Himself to us in the Bible, and through prayer we have direct access to Him with our problems and questions. We must learn how to pray and intercede. There are many good books that can help us in establishing a personal prayer life. We need to read them and learn from them so that through prayer we can spiritually sustain ourselves.

Likewise, there are many good Bible study guides that we can follow. Once Bible study is a regular part of our lives we will begin to reap the rewards of a more stable and mature relationship with the Lord. We will also have the personal confidence to go to the Bible and find our own answers to life's questions. God does not want us to be spiritually retarded and unable to sustain the new life He has given us. He wants us to reach a place of maturity where we can spiritually feed ourselves and be able to stand firm in the face of any adversity.

❒ It is God's will that we submit to governing authorities.

Submit yourselves for the Lord's sake to every human institution, whether to a king as the one in authority, or to governors sent by him for the punishment of evildoers and the praise of those who do right. For such is the will of God that by doing right you may silence the ignorance of foolish men (I Peter 2:13-15).

As long as the governing authorities are honest and unselfish, most of us can submit to them; but what about submitting to the laws of men that contradict the laws of God? At that point we must put God's laws above the laws of men. Absolute obedience is only given to God. Governments are ordained by God for the good of mankind, and when they exploit and abuse their responsibilities and the people they govern, they must be held accountable both to God and to the people they serve.

Obedience to the laws of God may lead us to disobey the laws of men, or to be in conflict with what we are asked to do by the rulers over us. We must be prepared as Christians to resist unrighteousness, corruption, prejudice, immortality, oppression, and every other form of evil. We should do that with love in our hearts, for the gospel is so radical that it commands us to love our enemies (Luke 6:32-36). That is what makes Christianity so powerful — we can submissively disobey, lovingly resist, passionately and intensely refuse to give in to evil men and corrupt systems, while we forgive those who are sinning against us.

❐ It is God's will that we grow through trials and adversity.

Consider it pure joy, my brothers, whenever you face trials of many kinds, because you know that the testing of your faith develops perseverance. Perseverance must finish its work so that you may be mature and complete, not lacking anything (James 1:2-4).

When faced with difficulties it is easy to question whether we really are in the will of God. But it is entirely possible to be in the will of God and still endure difficulties. Throughout our Christian life God will use difficult situations as a way of developing our characters, and we can never become mature Christians without them. There is no 'arm-chair correspondence course' for becoming a mature Christian — we must all go through struggles to get there. So, we must learn to embrace difficulties and trials as opportunities for developing spiritual muscle. We need these times and should not shy away from them. Don't pray for an easy life, pray for the strength to become a steadfast Christian.

My son, do not regard lightly the discipline of the Lord, nor faint when you are reproved by Him; For those whom the Lord loves He disciplines, and He encourages every son whom He receives' (Hebrews 12:5-6).

So that no one would be unsettled by these trials. You know quite well that we were destined for them' (I Thessalonians 3:3, NIV).

❐ It is God's will that we follow His Spirit rather than our selfish desires.

So as to live the rest of the time in the flesh no longer for the lusts of men, but for the will of God' (I Peter 4:2).

In life, we must choose to go in one of two directions. One direction has to do with the 'lusts of man', the other with doing 'the will of God'. The two are complete opposites. At one end of the scale we go our own way and enjoy what we consider to be the pleasures of life, and at the other end, we submit to the will of God and live our lives to please Him.

The word 'lust' is uses today mainly in relation to sex, but its meaning is much broader than that. To lust is to passionately or overwhelmingly desire something. We can lust for a higher paying job, a new car, stereo, or any physical thing. We can even lust to 'get even' with another person. Living life in this way is living according to the lusts of the flesh.

Jesus tells us that unless we deny ourselves, take up the cross and live for Him, we are not fit for His kingdom. This may seem harsh and uncompromising, but, given this world's condition, is the only alternative we have. If we choose to ignore Jesus, and continue living to fulfill the lusts of the flesh, our lives will be marked by confusion, disappointment, heartache, and ultimately destruction.

Most non-Christians are accustomed to living freely by their feelings. If they desire something, they go after it. As Christians we are taught in the Bible to make our choices based on truth, not on what feels good. When a person first becomes a Christian there can be a tremendous inner conflict between these two ways of living. If we are accustomed to living by our feelings, we will not 'feel good' about the Christian life, but if we persist in putting truth above pleasure, after a time we will find our pleasure from truth!

❒ It is God's will that we defend the rights of the poor.

Let us consider how to stimulate one another to love and good deeds, not forsaking our own assembling together, as is the habit of some, but encouraging one another; and all the more, as you see the day drawing near (Hebrews 10:24-25).

❒ It is God's will for us to do justice and to love mercy.

He has shown you, O man, what is good. And what does the Lord require of you? To act justly and love mercy, to walk humbly with your God (Micah 6:8).

We live in a world that is filled with injustice and inequality. As Christians, God calls us to make sure nothing we do contributes to the exploitation of those who are defenseless and poor (James 1:27, 5:1-6). In fact, we are commanded to defend the rights of the poor (Psalm 82:3). Because they are defenseless, we are to defend them (Proverbs 31:9). This will mean that at times there will, of necessity, be confrontation with those who oppress the poor. It is inevitable if we are defending those who are the victims of greed or oppression.

Because poverty creates hopelessness and lack of power over one's own life, a certain listlessness and apathy can result. It is dangerous to judge people quickly when they appear to be lazy. Perhaps they are suffering from the results of poor motivation, ignorance, despair, or bad parenting. Raising people out of such poverty requires great patience and mercy. That is one reason why the Lord commands us to 'love mercy'.

Further, 'doing justice' and 'loving mercy' does not mean we have all the answers. A paternalistic approach to the poor says as much about our needs as the needs of others. We have much to learn from all people. If we are to serve others we must not decide what their problems are and then impose our solutions. We are to serve all men from a basis of relationship. If we are not willing to take time to develop genuine friendships with the oppressed and poor in society, we should not try to get involved in their lives. We could do more harm than good.

❒ It is God's will for us to love and forgive those who offend us.

That all of them may be one, Father, just as you are in me, and I am in you. May they also be in us so that the world may believe that you have sent me.

I have given them the glory that you gave me that they may be one as we are one. I in them and you in me.

May they be brought to complete unity to let the world know that you sent me and have loved them even as you have loved me (John 17:21-23).

continued on page 45

The Necessity Of PRAYER

by Edward M. Bounds

Editor's Note:

We consider E.M. Bounds to be one of the greatest teachers in recent church history on the crucial subject of prayer. Though he passed away at the beginning of the twentieth century his writings will not cease to speak and prepare the church for her ultimate destiny.

The following is a condensed excerpt from Mr Bounds work by the same title. The entire series of Bounds works on prayer has been published by Baker Book House of Grand Rapids, MI. and is available in most Christian bookstores.

PRAYER & FAITH

"A dear friend of mine who was quite a lover of the chase told me the following story: 'Rising early one morning,' he said, 'I heard the baying of a score of deerhounds in pursuit of their quarry. Looking away to a broad, open field in front of me, I saw a young fawn making its way across, and giving signs, moreover, that its race was well-nigh run. Reaching the rails of the enclosure, it leaped over and crouched within ten feet from where I stood. A moment later when two of the hounds came over, the fawn ran in my direction and pushed its head between my legs. I lifted the little thing to my breast and, swinging round and round, fought off the dogs. I felt, just then, that all the dogs in the West could not, and should not capture that fawn after its weakness had appealed to my strength.' So it is, when human helplessness appeals to Almighty God. Well do I remember when the hounds of sin were after my soul until, at last, I ran into the arms of Almighty God."

—*A.C. Dixon*

In the principles of prayer, first place must be given to faith. It is the initial quality in the heart of any man who would to talk to the Unseen. He must stretch forth hands of faith. He must believe, where he cannot prove. In the ultimate issue, prayer is simply faith, claiming its natural yet marvelous prerogatives — faith taking possession of its illimitable inheritance. True godliness is just as true, steady, and persevering in the realm of faith as it is in the province of prayer. When faith ceases to pray, it ceases to live.

Faith does the impossible because it brings God to undertake for us, and nothing is impossible with God. How great — without qualification or limitation — is the power of faith! If doubt be banished from the heart, and unbelief made a stranger there, what we ask of God shall surely come to pass, and a believer hath vouchsafed to him "whatsoever he saith."

Prayer projects faith on God, and God on the world. Only God can move mountains, but faith and prayer move God. In His cursing of the fig-tree our Lord demonstrated His power. Following that, He proceeded to declare, that large powers were committed to faith and prayer, not in order to kill but to make alive, not to blast but to bless.

At this point in our study, we turn to a saying of our Lord, which there is need to emphasize, since it is the very keystone of the arch of faith and prayer.

> "Therefore I say unto you, What things soever ye desire when ye pray, believe that ye receive them, and ye shall have them."

We should ponder well that statement — "Believe that ye receive them, and ye shall have them." Here is described a faith which realizes, which appropriates, which takes. Such faith is a consciousness of the Divine, an experienced communion, a realized certainty.

Is faith growing or declining as the years go by? Does faith stand strong these days as iniquity abounds and the love of many grows cold? Does faith maintain its hold, as religion tends to become a mere formality and worldliness increasingly prevails? The enquiry of our Lord, may, with great appropriateness, be ours. "When the Son of Man cometh," He asks, "shall He find faith on the earth?" We believe that He will, and it is ours, in this day, to see to it that the lamp of faith is trimmed and burning.

Faith is the foundation of Christian character and the security of the soul. When Jesus was looking forward to Peter's denial, and cautioning him against it, He said unto His disciple:

> "Simon, Simon, behold, Satan hath desired to have you, to sift you as wheat; but I have prayed for thee, that thy faith fail not."

Our Lord was declaring a central truth; it was Peter's faith He was seeking to guard; for He knew that when faith is broken down, the foundations of spiritual life give way, and the entire structure of religious experience falls. It was Peter's faith which needed guarding. Hence Christ's solicitude for the welfare of His disciple's soul and His determination to fortify Peter's faith by His own all-prevailing prayer.

In his "Second Epistle", Peter has this idea in mind when speaking of growth in grace as a measure of safety in the Christian life, and as implying fruitfulness.

> "And besides this," he declared, "giving diligence, add to your faith virtue; and to virtue knowledge; and to knowledge temperance' and to temperance patience; and to patience godliness."

Of this process, faith was the starting-point — the basis of the other graces of the Spirit. Faith was the foundation on which other things were to be built. Peter does not enjoin his readers to add to works or gifts or virtues but to faith. Much depends on starting right in this business of growing in grace. There is a Divine order, of which Peter was aware; and so he goes on to declare that we are to give diligence to making our calling and election sure, which election is rendered certain adding to faith which, in turn, is done by constant, earnest praying. Thus faith is kept alive by prayer, and every step taken, in this adding of grace to grace, is accompanied by prayer.

The faith which creates powerful praying is the faith which centers itself on a powerful Person. Faith in Christ's ability to do and to do greatly, is the faith which prays greatly. Thus the leper lay hold upon the power of Christ. "Lord, if Thou wilt," he cried, "Thou canst make me clean." In this instance, we are shown how faith centered in Christ's ability to do, and how it secured the healing power.

It was concerning this very point, that Jesus questioned the blind men who came to Him for healing:

> "Believe ye that I am able to do this?" He asks. "They

> said unto Him, Yea, Lord. Then touched He their eyes, saying, According to your faith be it unto you."

It was to inspire faith in His ability to do that Jesus left behind Him, that last, great statement, which, in the final analysis, is a ringing challenge to faith. "All power," He declared, "is given unto Me in heaven and in earth."

Again: faith is obedient; it goes when commanded, as did the nobleman, who came to Jesus, in the day of His flesh, and whose son was grievously sick.

Moreover: such faith acts. Like the man who was born blind, it goes to wash in the pool of Siloam when told to wash. Like Peter on Gennesaret it casts the net where Jesus commands, instantly, without question or doubt. Such faith takes away the stone from the grave of Lazarus promptly. A praying faith keeps the commandments of God and does those things which are well pleasing in His sight. It asks, "Lord, what wilt Thou have me to do?" and answers quickly, "Speak, Lord, Thy servant heareth." Obedience helps faith, and faith, in turn, helps obedience. To do God's will is essential to true faith, and faith is necessary to implicit obedience.

Yet faith is called upon often to wait in patience before God, and is prepared for God's seeming delays in answering

❦

E.M. BOUNDS

Edward McKendree Bounds did not merely pray well that he might write well about prayer. He prayed because the needs of the world were upon him. He prayed, for long years, upon subjects which the easy-going Christian rarely gave a thought, and for objects which men of less thought and faith are always ready to call impossible. From his solitary, prayer-vigils, year by year, there arose teaching equaled by few men is modern Christian history. He wrote transcendently about prayer, because he was himself, transcendent in its practice.

As breathing is a physical reality to us so prayer was a reality to Bounds. He took the command, "Pray without ceasing" almost as literally as animate nature takes the law of the reflex nervous system, which controls our breathing.

Prayer-books—real text-books, not forms of prayer—were the fruit of this daily spiritual exercise. Not brief articles for the religious press came from his pen—though he had been experienced in that field for years—not pamphlets, but books were the product and result. He was hindered by poverty, obscurity, loss of prestige, yet his victory was not wholly reserved until his death. In 1907, he gave to the world two small editions. One of these was widely circulated in Great Britain. The years following up to his death in 1913 were filled with constant labour and he went home to God leaving a collection of manuscripts. His letters carry the request that the present editor should publish these products of his gifted pen.

The preservation of the Bounds manuscripts to the present time has clearly been providential. The work of preparing them for the press has been a labour of love, consuming years of effort.

These books are unfailing wells for a lifetime of spiritual water-drawing. They are hidden treasures, wrought in the darkness of the dawn and the heat of the noon, on the anvil of experience, and beaten into wondrous form by the mighty stroke of the Divine. They are living voices whereby he, being dead, yet speaketh. ❦

— Claude Chilton, Jr.

prayer. Faith does not grow disheartened because prayer is not immediately honored; it takes God at His Word, and lets Him take what time He chooses to fulfill His purposes. There is bound to be much delay and long days of waiting for true faith, but faith accepts the conditions — knows there will be delays in answering prayer, and regards such delays as times of testing, in the which, it is privileged to show its mettle, and the stern stuff of which it is made.

The case of Lazarus was an instance of where there was delay, where the faith of two good women was sorely tried: Lazarus was critically ill, and his sisters sent for Jesus. But, our Lord delayed His going to the relief of His sick friend. The plea was urgent — "Lord, behold, he whom Thou lovest is sick," — but the Master is not moved by it. Furthermore: our Lord's tardiness appeared to bring about hopeless disaster. While Jesus tarried, Lazarus died. But the delay of Jesus was exercised in the interests of a greater good. Finally, He makes His way to the home in Bethany.

> "Then said Jesus unto them plainly, Lazarus is dead. And I am glad for your sakes, that I was not there, to the intent ye may believe; nevertheless let us go unto him."

Fear not, O tempted and tried believer, Jesus will come, if patience be exercised, and faith hold fast. His delay will serve to make His coming the more richly blessed. Pray on. Wait on. Thou canst not fail. If Christ delay, wait for Him. In His own good time, He will come, and will not tarry.

Delay is often the test and the strength of faith. How much patience is required when these times of testing come! Yet faith gathers strength by waiting and praying. Patience has its perfect work in the school of delay. In some instances, delay is of the very essence of the prayer. God has to do many things, antecedent to giving the final answer — things which are essential to the lasting good of him who is requesting favour at His hands.

Jacob prayed, with point and ardor, to be delivered from Esau. But before that prayer could be answered, there was much to be done with, and for Jacob. He must be changed, as well as Esau. Jacob had to be made into a new man, before Esau could be. Jacob had to be converted to God, before Esau could be converted to Jacob.

Among the large and luminous utterances of Jesus concerning prayer, none is more arresting than this:

> "Verily, verily, I say unto you, He that believeth on Me, the works that I do shall he do also; and greater works than these shall he do; because I go unto My Father.
>
> And whatsoever ye shall ask in My Name, that will I do, that the Father may be glorified in the Son. If ye shall ask anything in My Name, I will do it."

Faith in Christ is the basis of all working, and of all praying. All wonderful works depend on wonderful praying, and all praying is done in the Name of Jesus Christ. Amazing lesson, of wondrous simplicity, is this praying in the name of the Lord Jesus! All other conditions are depreciated, everything else is renounced, save Jesus only. The name of Christ — the Person of our Lord and Saviour Jesus Christ — must be supremely sovereign, in the hour and article of prayer.

If Jesus dwells at the fountain of my life; if the currents of His life have displaced and superseded all self-currents; if implicit obedience to Him be the inspiration and force of every movement of my life, then He can safely commit the praying to my will, and pledge Himself, by an obligation as profound as His own nature, that whatsoever is asked shall be granted. Nothing can be clearer, more distinct, more unlimited both in application and extent, than the exhortation and urgency of Christ, "Have faith in God."

Faith covers temporal as well as spiritual needs. Faith dispels all undue anxiety and needless care about what shall

continued on page 44

Finding Spiritual Safety

by Paul Cain

We are living in a powerful day in which God is increasing the manifestation of His Spirit through the church to our world. Along with this precious work of our Lord is an effort by Satan to discredit what God is doing by bringing an increase in the manifestations of false gifts, deception and the supernatural power of the kingdom of darkness. This effort to distort and discredit by the enemy is given access in the church through ignorance, immaturity and carnality.

Along with this wonderful increase in the outpouring of the Holy Spirit, God is wanting to restore the ministry office of the prophet to the Body of Christ. These efforts of our Lord often meet resistance by Christian leaders because of the obvious problems created by fleshly imitations and even demonic expressions that Satan brings to discredit what God is doing. These Christian leaders have an oversight responsibility to guard the flock and protect them from danger, while leading them to feed on the Lord.

This is why *spiritual safety* is such an important issue today. Every Christian and every Pastor wants to be guided by the Lord and wants to have spiritual safety in the leadings they sense, the counsel they give or receive, and in the operation of the gifts of the Holy Spirit that flow to or through their lives.

God has made a full provision for safety in our lives so that we can receive what He is doing without fear and filter out the efforts of the enemy to distract, imitate and discredit the precious work of our Lord.

As we take an overview of the patterns of safety that God has provided for us, we need to recognize that these patterns of safety all tie together to form a *safety net* under our life and ministry. In correct application these patterns are all related and interdependent. In this way, if one strand fails due to imperfections, others remain to hold us secure in the middle of God's will. "For you, Lord, only make me dwell in safety" (Psalm 4:8).

Spiritual safety begins with a total commitment to the Lordship and leadership of Jesus Christ in our life. Without a commitment to His leadership, we are automatically disqualifying ourselves from the spiritual safety He is seeking to give us. Submission to His leadership, where and how it is manifested, including proper relationships of accountability to proven ministries, is His canopy of safety. "...Whoso hearkens unto me shall dwell in safety and shall be quiet from fear of evil" (Proverbs 1:33). "Wherefore you shall do my statutes, and keep my judgments, and do them; and you shall dwell in the land in safety. And the land shall yield her fruit, and you shall eat your fill, and dwell therein in safety" (Leveticus 25:18-19).

Safety is a place where you are protected from danger. The guidelines and boundaries provided by a place of safety keep you from danger. If you step outside of them, you enter an area that can be destructive.

As we glance over the following patterns of safety, we will begin to learn how to judge personal leadership, counsel, and manifestations of the Spirit, as to whether they are of God, of man, or of the devil.

The first principle of safety is that all ministry is to be **subject to the written Word of God**. It is error to exalt experience above the Word, for only by the Word can we correctly interpret our experience. Submission to God's authority is also submission to the full discipline of the written Word. If we want the full expression of the Lord, we must be committed to what is genuine and nothing less. Truth will always stand up under investigation. We must allow the written Word and the church to critically investigate the source of every leading, counsel, and manifestation of the Spirit. "The fear of man brings a snare; but whosoever puts his trust in the Lord shall be safe" (Proverbs 29:25.

We live in a culture that highly esteems independence, but there should be no independent spirit when it comes to interpreting the scriptures. II Peter 1:20 says "But know this first of all, that no prophecy of scripture is a matter of one's own interpretation".

Every body of literature has "laws of interpretation" which are called hermeneutics. These laws are inherent to the use of language to communicate and provide a solid platform for understanding. For example, one of these laws is: never take a verse out of context. Never use one isolated scripture to build a doctrine. Context involves a number of things such as the context of the verses in a passage, the book it is found in , the culture of the day, who is speaking to whom, etc. There are many basic principles of hermaneutics which can be used to keep us on the path to sound Biblical interpretation. We must believe that if we are to submit to the Word that there is a dependable, valid interpretation for us that is reliable. Let us remember, however, that as we walk with the Living Word that the revelation of God in scripture is never given as disemination of information. It is always given in the context of circumstances, needs or conditions where the revelation is applicable. "All scripture is given by inspiration of God, and is profitable for doctrine, for reproof, for correction, for instruction in righteousness" (II Timothy 3:16).

A second principle of safety is for the expressions of the Spirit to be **subject to and confirmed by the oversight ministries of the church**. Proper relationships with the body of Christ brings accountability and protection from one's own blind spots. Such a relationship of transparency and inspection is not a lording over and dictating direction in another's life. It is, however, a responsible speaking into the lives of one another to bring awareness and to check for the genuine. Scripture teaches that God holds leaders accountable for the spiritual health and welfare of the flock. "Obey them that have rule over you, and submit yourselves: for they watch for your souls, as they must give account, that they may do it with joy, and not with gief: for that is unprofitable for you" (Hebrews 13:17).

Those in authority are responsible to correct, rebuke, and admonish to establish the believer in truth, but this does not mean that leaders are supposed to know the will of God for every situation or individual in their care. The leader's responsibility is to help those in his charge determine the will of God for themselves while maintaining sound Biblical principles for guidance. Responsibility does not require control; it requires leadership. "Not that we have dominion over your faith, but are helpers of your joy: for by faith you stand" (II Corinthians 1:24).

Saying that God's appointed leaders do not have *dominion* does not mean that they do not have the authority to bring correction, reproof and to protect the household of faith from disorder, sin and destructive influences, as they have been given the wisdom to understand. If we are wise we will embrace reproof or correction. The one who has come to know the Good Shepherd will receive comfort from the rod and staff (Psalm 23:4). "He that refuses instruction despises his own soul. He that hears reproof gets understanding" (Proverbs 15:32).

Many of the questions most of us face have already been experienced and handled by those in authority. Therefore they can give wisdom and instruction that can save us from error. It is a joy and marvelous provision from the Lord to have men and women who have "through faith and patience" inherited the promises, to whom we can go and receive help and guidance. We can recognize His truly appointed leaders as those who have attained the promises, those who manifest the fruit and power of the Holy Spirit in their own lives. As the writer of Hebrews exhorts: "Remember those who led you, who spoke the word of God to you; *and considering the result of their conduct, imitate their faith* (Hebrews 13:7).

The wise saint will not try to avoid the counsel of the elders, but will search out the wisdom of those who have gone before him. Proverbs 11:14 says, "Where there is no counsel the people fall, but in the multitude of counselors there is safety." We are in a spiritual war, and Proverbs 24:6 instructs: "For by wise counsel thou shalt make war, and in the multitude of counselors there is safety." We do not need to avoid counselors, *but to search diligently for them!*

The Lord does not give authority without accountability. He was the first to establish checks and balances within His government. Every realm of authority has accountability patterns established by Him: child-parent, husband-wife, employer-employee, etc. When we rebel against the authorities He has established we are in fact rebelling against Him. Would a wise father give the keys to a powerful new car to a son he could not trust? Let us not expect to receive spiritual authority and power if we are not in proper submission to Him, by His written word, or in the body of Christ.

A third basic principle for spiritual safety is the **devotion to integrity**. If we are to walk in truth we need to be honest about what we know, and about what we do not know. Integrity comes from the desire to walk in the will of God, to be intimate with Him and to please Him in all things. It is when we depart from the simplicity of devotion to Him to try and please ourselves, men, or even the demonic forces of fear, greed, lust, etc., that we depart from integrity. That departure usually proceeds from exaggeration to outright deception.

The kingdom of God is built upon the foundation of truth; it cannot be established or its purposes furthered by exaggerations or false witness. Even if we do it for the purpose of trying to further the work of God, exaggerations detract from the kingdom by eroding our integrity, which sooner or later will lead to our deception. Scripture testifies that "The integrity of the upright shall guide them" (Proverbs 11:3) and "Unto the upright there arises light in the darkness" (Psalm 112:4).

Five good biblical illustrations of integrity as a means of safety in keeping one in the will of God are:

1 **ABRAHAM** refused to share the spoils after the battle of the kings. Abraham was determined that if he was going to receive wealth or power it would not be by man's hand but by God's. *Integrity honors God as the Source.*

2 **BOAZ and RUTH** had a commitment to deal rightly by their relatives that enabled them to become direct ancestors of King David and thereby ancestors of the Lord Jesus. If we are to bear fruit that is Christ we must do right by our brothers. *Integrity honors our brothers.*

3 **JOSEPH** had so much integrity that he would not take advantage of his prominence to wrong the authority over him (his master). Even though this integrity cost him his temporary freedom, it ultimately resulted in his being trusted with the highest position of authority in the kingdom. *Integrity honors those who are in authority over us.*

4 **ESTHER** had integrity so as not to use her position as queen just to please or lookout for herself, but she risked her life to save her people. God honored her by devoting an entire book of the Bible to her story. *Integrity honors those who are under our authority.*

5 **DAVID** had integrity so that he would not offer to God that which cost him nothing (I Kings 24:24). *Integrity will always pay the full price to be obedient.*

There are several other principles of safety that help form the safety net under our lives. These inlcude learning to know the witenss of the Holy Spirit, finding confirmation in the circumstances of life, and understanding how to cooperate with the manifestation s of the Holy Spirit in our life.

In conclusion, it is important not to confuse the gifts of the Holy spirit and the gifts of the Son, the gift of prophecy and the office of the Prophet. Paul wrote the Corinthian Church about the gifts of the Holy spirit saying, "For you may all prophecy one by one, that all may learn, and may be comforted" (I Corinthians 14:31). However, this is very distinct from the office of a Prophet as given by the ascended Son of God (Ephesians 4:8-11).

In this present move of the Spirit, God is wnating to restore the office of the Prophet, and the enemy wants to rob the body of christ of this needed ministry by bringing in the false. The best way to expose th false is for the genuine to rise! This will take place as Chritian leaders learn to understand the patern of safety in the scriptures and apply them to both manifestation of th Spirit and offices of ministry in our day. ■

As a young man Paul Cain almost instantly attained national prominence as an evangelist who displayed uncommon prophetic gifts and authority over disease. Barely in his twenties, he often filled his 10,000 seat tent and began to impact major cities with the gospel. Then, at the height of his ministry, he was compelled by the Lord to return to obscurity. He was then given a promise that if he would keep himself pure from the corruptions of self-promotion and gain that the Lord would use him to help anoint a "last day ministry." As a sign of this promise the Lord said that He would keep Paul's mother alive until he had met members of this last day ministry—she passed away in April of 1990 at the age of 104. Almost immediately Paul Cain has again emerged as a significant voice to the church. Even though Paul often displays extraordinary prophetic gifts and power, he has become known just as much for his humility, integrity, devotion to truth and pure devotion to the Lord—these too being signs that a last day ministry is arising.

LET THE BATTLE BEGIN

by Rick Joyner

On New Years Eve I saw storm clouds in the spirit from which there could be no escape. As the storm was about to break a voice said "Psalm 91 is for 1991." Even though we may not be able to escape the storm we do have shelter in the midst of it. Even as all of the kingdoms of this world begin to shake we have a kingdom that cannot be shaken. As the Lord Jesus Himself declared:

> **Therefore everyone who hears these words of Mine, *and acts upon them*, may be compared to a wise man, who built his house upon the rock.**
>
> And the rain descended and the floods came, and the winds blew, and burst against that house; and yet it did not fall, for it had been founded upon the rock.
>
> And everyone who hears these words of Mine and does not act upon them, will be like a foolish man, who built his house upon the sand.
>
> And the rain descended, and the floods came, and the winds blew, and burst against that house; and it fell, and great was its fall (Matthew 7:24-27).

What is happening in the natural is but a reflection of what is happening in the spirit. The "prince of Persia" is one of the strongest principalities on earth. It is determined to assert its authority and take dominion, ultimately of the whole earth. Even though this conflict is reflected in earthly battles the real battle is spiritual, in the heavenlies. We will not have a breakthrough until the body of Christ, like Daniel, prays and fasts with zeal and focused vision for the restoration of His temple (that is not made with human hands, but is made out of human beings) and the heavenly Jerusalem, whose restoration will be reflected by the ingrafting of the earthly Jerusalem.

The body of Christ must prepare for this war spiritually like an army would prepare for battle in the natural. We must get rid of our excess baggage. **"No Soldier in active service entangles himself in the affairs of everyday life, so that he may please the one who enlisted him as a soldier" (II Timothy 2:4).** We must:

1. Get rid of the sin and spiritual pollution in our life.
2. Get rid of those "good" things which distract us from our spiritual calling.
3. Get out of debt and do not make major purchases without a clear leading from the Lord. Debt is one of the world's strongest and most effective yokes in keeping God's people restrained and unable to follow Him. It keeps us in the control of human pressures and unable to move by the Spirit. For over twenty years the Lord has been giving His people a clear warning to get out of debt; those who have not heeded are about to be overcome by the flood He has been trying to prepare us for. If you have been disobedient in this start moving *today* to be obedient and He will help you. (Read and heed **I Timothy 6:3-19**).

After we have thrown off these yokes we must:

1. Seek first the kingdom of God. (**Matthew 6:25-34**)
2. Take on the full armor of God. (**Ephesians 6:10-18**)

There will be no victory without a battle. This war is a righteous war; it is a holy war. But we do not war against flesh and blood. The foundational stronghold of the prince of Persia is ***racism***. The body of Christ has no authority over this spirit if it has dominion in our own lives. In Christ the dividing walls are taken down. God loves the Arabs and we must love them and pray for them, not against them. The Lord Jesus came to save men not destroy them. Pray for the salvation of the Arab people and the Jewish people. Prayer is more powerful than any bomb; praise is more powerful than politics. Pray for the bringing down of every stronghold that exalts itself against the true knowledge of God. ■

The Magnificence of GOD

by John G. Elliott

The revival of worship expressed through praise and thanksgiving is gaining momentum as we approach the close of the twentieth century. Because of the obvious infusion of life it brings, even a significant number of denominational churches generally considered "traditional" are now showing an increasing interest in the less restrained and more prolonged expressions of adoration to God. Although there is yet widespread resistance to this current work of God, there are encouraging signs of hope.

There is a growing number of theologically conservative leaders who are confessing a sense of dryness in their worship services. There is now a greater uneasiness than ever before with the traditional two hymns followed by the offering and the sermon. In the days ahead this backdrop of barrenness will drive many to the oasis of the presence of the living God whose habitation is found in the praises of His people!

From the other side of the spectrum there are many pastors and leaders who have believed that their worship services were "Spirit-led" but who are now admitting that "form" has been squeezing out real Life. Expressions of worship given birth by the Spirit in years past have had a tendency to become routine through the passage of time. Traditions are not always bad, but when they become a form of godliness without power we must turn away from them. Even congregations who have considered themselves "non-traditional" have seen their worship become stale and lifeless. The last three great movements in the church, the Pentecostal, the Charismatic and the Third Wave all tried to resist becoming mere traditions but today there is the "Pentecostal tradition" of worship, the "Charismatic tradition" and the "Third Wave" tradition. It is our natural tendency to move from the new wineskin of Life toward the old, inflexible wineskin of a subtle religious form.

One solution to this problem, simple yet profound, is to simply see our God as He is. Our God is overwhelmingly great! The foundational building block of Spirit-led praise is stated clearly in Psalm 145:3: "Great is the Lord and most worthy of praise, **His greatness no one can fathom**. When we see Him as He truly is, we will not only worship, but we will do so with a sense of awe! The thrill of worship belongs to those who see Him in His majestic splendor and in the vast array of His supreme and awesome characteristics. Although there are other factors involved which may hinder true worship, the primary hindrance lies in our failure to see Him in His glory.

As we fix our eyes upon Him who is the true author of our faith we will avoid the dangerous tendency of worshipping the worship experience itself. If He is at the center of our attention we will cease from pursuing a self-focused gratification from the worship assembly and turn to seek Him and Him alone.

The essence of true worship is found in the very greatness and worthiness of God Himself. Therefore, it is our role to **magnify** Him. In order to magnify God we must amplify and enlarge our understanding of His characteristics, qualities and actions. His ways and His thoughts must become the object of our attention. Even as an astronomer uses a telescope to magnify a distant galaxy, so we must exercise a similar activity in our worship. It is not God who needs to be enlarged. It is our perception of Him that needs to be expanded. "Great are the works of the Lord, they are 'pondered' by all who delight in them. Glorious and majestic are His deeds" (Psalm 111:2,3). "I remember the days of long ago; I 'meditate' on all Your works and consider what Your hands have done" (Psalm 143:5). In these and many other passages the true worshipper is characterized by a life of pondering, considering and meditating.

In Psalm 139 David sets an example for us when he looks at the unique configuration of his own body, soul and spirit and declares, "I praise You because I am fearfully and wonderfully made; Your works are wonderful, I know that full well! (verse 14). Consider the creative ingenuity of Him who placed within the human body 222 bones, 636 muscles and millions of cells with thousands of unique functions, all performing their tasks within the context of five major systems. The nervous system alone contains over 2000 miles of nerve fiber and is controlled by the brain which performs functions unequalled by the most sophisticated computers on earth! The eye itself contains over 107 million cells. Seven million of those cells are called cones which fire off messages to the brain when a few photons of light cross them. These cones make it possible to distinguish 1000 shades of color. The other 100 million cells are rods and can distinguish a spectrum of light so broad that the most brilliant light perceived is a billion times greater than the dullest light. The human ear is marvelous to ponder. The three tiny bones of the ear can detect sound frequencies that flutter the eardrum as faintly as one billionth of a centimeter (a distance one tenth the diameter of a hydrogen atom).

How amazing He is! Who has known the mind of the Lord or has understood a fraction of His immense knowledge? We are surrounded by innumerable examples of His creative power. We constantly step on or brush by or overlook His awesome deeds. Consider the earth on which He has placed us. The moon, which is the closest celestial body to ours, does not have one single living cell on it, yet just one simple block of forest soil, one foot square by one inch deep, contains "an average of 1,356 living creatures, including 865 mites, 265 springtails, 22 millipedes, 19 adult beetles, and various numbers of 12 other forms", not to mention another two million bacteria and the millions of fungi and algae discernable only by an electron microscope. It is our awesome God who created the heavens and the earth and all it contains! He knows the number and location of all these tiny creatures, as well as the moment they come into existence and the instant they depart. Who is like our God? Who could ever trace out His pathways?!

The writer of Proverbs advises us to consider the ways of the ant. This fascinating creature, though small by human standards, is able to lift sixty to eighty times its own body weight. The ant is unsurpassed in diligence and in her ability to labor tirelessly for the good of her colony. Even in creatures such as this we recognize the ingenuity and worthiness of our Creator.

Ponder the heavens! His glory is recorded across the starlit sky. Even many unbelievers express a sense of awe when placed beneath the silent heavens. How much more should we who know the Creator Himself proclaim unending adoration at His marvelous creativity and unsearchable knowledge! A small amount of pondering on a clear night will tend to produce a large amount of genuine praise!

The nearest star to the planet earth is our own

sun. It is about 93 million miles away. Light travels at a speed of 186,000 miles per second (about seven times around the equator). When we observe a sunset we are watching history—it actually took place eight minutes before we had the experience of viewing it. The next nearest star to us is Alpha Centuari at a distance of four light years. (A light year is the distance light travels in one year.) Imagine spending the next four years of your life traveling at the speed of light in order to arrive at that solitary star! Consider also that the galaxy we live in (the Milky Way) contains 100 billion stars. The diameter of the Milky Way Galaxy is 100,000 light years! Scientists now estimate that there are about 100 billion galaxies in the universe and that it is rapidly expanding! It is as though our God is so overwhelmingly great that He continues to create new and vast regions of outer space, filling them with stars, planets and galaxies while simultaneously sustaining the billions of tiny cells within one human body.

The Lady Julian, who lived in medieval times, was known for her dreams and visions of God. On one occasion she saw the Lord walking about heaven holding a tiny object in His hand. The object was about the size of a peanut. Furthermore, she could easily see that God gave it constant attention as though it were a priceless treasure. She dared to ask Him the question, "Lord, what do You hold in Your hand?" His reply astounded her. "This is **everything** I have made!"

Is He not worthy of praise?! All the worship of an eternal lifetime would not be sufficient to declare the excellency of our awesome God! Every creature in heaven and on earth, ranging from the most splendid cherubim to the lowliest member of the animal kingdom, singing together with the stars themselves, could never generate enough volume in triumphant jubilation to proclaim His greatness!

Moreover, ponder His sublime characteristics. Who is like Him? He is everlasting in love, boundless in mercy, absolute in power, immaculate in perfection, endless in understanding, perfect in righteousness, terrible in wrath, infinite in wisdom, unsearchable in knowledge, brilliant in splendor, just in judgment, inexhaustible in patience, astounding in humility and all-encompassing in holiness. He dwells in unapproachable light.

His thoughts are immeasurable. His peace is beyond understanding. His joy is indescribable. His mercy is new and fresh every morning. He holds the vast created universe within the palm of His hand! **Who compares with Him?!** He is the most exciting being that could ever be imagined! His greatness far exceeds our imagination even as the rapidly expanding universe exceeds a tiny grain of sand.

Ponder His eternal plans! Consider the incarnation, the crucifixion, the resurrection, the plan of salvation, the covenants, the Word of God, the heavenly host and a vast array of other subjects; who can begin to comprehend the deep mysteries of His mind?

One of the supreme joys we will know in heaven is being able to spend eternity plumbing the depths of His greatness. Yet, after ages of research and learning, we will never be able to say that we have exhausted our study of Him and His deeds. To the contrary we will joyfully declare that we have come to know but a fraction of His unfathomable greatness!

We must keep Him at the center of the viewing screen. Let us fix our eyes upon Jesus, the Author and Finisher of our faith (Hebrews 12:2). "Come, let us **magnify** the Lord and let us exalt His Name together!" (Psalm 34:3) ■

John Elliott has been devoted to music since childhood. After attaining a Master of Arts in New Testament Studies, John served as a campus minister at Purdue University. In 1982 John began to write songs and produce records. His songs have been recorded by some of the top Christian artists including Pat Boone, Sandi Patti, Steve Green and others. His own recent release "Let All The Thirst Come" promises to be a significant contribution to the new direction coming to Christian Music.

SECONDHAND SAINTS

WILL OUR CHILDREN REALLY KNOW JESUS?

by Bob and Jim Buchan

Jesus' disciples had no trouble answering when He asked them what people were saying as to His identity. "Some say John the Baptist; others say Elijah; and still others, Jeremiah or one of the prophets."

> "Who do you say that I am?" He asked.
>
> Simon Peter answered, "You are the Christ, the Son of the living God!"
>
> Jesus replied, "Blessed are you, Simon son of Jonah, for this was not revealed to you by man, but by my Father in Heaven." (Matthew 16:13-20).

Peter was truly a "first generation" follower of Jesus. His knowledge of who Jesus is was not gained by taking a public opinion poll or by attending a Sunday school class, but by having a personal revelation from God. The crucial nature of having this personal knowledge of the Lord can be seen in Jesus' prayer to the Father: Now this is eternal life; that they may KNOW YOU, the only true God, and Jesus Christ, whom you have sent." (John 17:3).

Unless we know Him we don't have eternal life.

A GENERATION WHO DIDN'T KNOW THE LORD

In all generations, it has been God's desire to have people who know Him and want to have fellowship with Him. Yet in Judges, chapter 2, after commenting that the people had served the Lord during the time of Joshua and during the time of the elders who survived Joshua, it is stated "...there arose another generation after them who did not know the Lord, nor the work which he had done for Israel" (Judges 2:7,10). Surely they had HEARD of the Lord and His great work for their forefathers, but their knowledge of Him was only secondhand.

The generations that followed Joshua did not have to pay a price for the inheritance they had received. The "Promised Land" was something they grew up in and took for granted. Neither work nor warfare on their part was necessary to gain the land of milk and honey so they consequently failed to appreciate what they had.

Today we observe this same tendency in the kids of America who have had everything they ever wanted (in terms of money and material possessions) handed to them on a silver platter. Parents often wonder why their children seem ungrateful, concluding that "kids today are just unappreciative." The truth is that we usually don't place a high value on things we obtain without personal sacrifice.

The generation that sprung up after Joshua's valiant fight for the Promised Land had no firsthand experience with God Himself and His miraculous provision. Rather, they found themselves simply inheriting a position of strength and prosperity in Canaan, tempting them to lose their dependence on God and the very thing He had warned them about:

Beware that you don't forget the Lord your God...Otherwise you may say in your heart,

"My power and the might of my hand have gotten me this wealth" (Deuteronomy 8:11,17).

The Book of Judges then records a series of instances where God allowed Israel to be overcome by its enemies. Finding themselves again in a position of weakness, the people had no option but to cry out to the Lord for deliverance. In response, God faithfully raised up leaders to demonstrate His constant love and miracle-working power.

We have witnessed a great outpouring of the Holy Spirit in this generation and in many ways have beheld the great and mighty acts of God. Yet there is a crucial need for our children, and those we lead to the Lord, to also have a firsthand exposure to the power of God, and not just give mental assent to the things we pass on to them. Our natural children and our spiritual children must also see the cost involved in following Christ — for they will not truly appreciate something they inherit on a silver platter.

DAVID AND SOLOMON

An interesting example of this "second generation" effect can be seen in the lives of David and his son, Solomon. David was a man after God's heart, and in the latter years of his life he had a strong vision to see a glorious temple constructed to house the Ark of the covenant. (I Chronicles 17; Psalms 4:132). But the Lord told him that his son would build the temple rather than he himself. Nevertheless, David took great pains to make adequate preparations for the future construction. (I Chronicles 22).

After his father's death, Solomon seems to have begun his reign with a real knowledge of God and a desire to obey Him, (I Kings 11:1-11).

An important lesson that can be learned from Solomon's fall is this: he continued to serve the Lord faithfully as long as he was pursuing his father's dream of building the temple. But the vision was really David's, and the sacrifice of preparation was David's — Solomon just had to carry out the plan.

The problem is that after his father's plan was completed, Solomon had NO VISION OF HIS OWN. We can only follow someone else's revelation and vision for so long and then we will begin to drift away unless we have a fresh word from God for our own life. (Proverbs 29:18).

SPIRITUALITY WITHOUT SACRIFICE

It is almost too easy to gain an intellectual education in the Bible in our country today. All we have to do is send for a study outline from our favorite radio preacher, or listen to cassette tapes, or read a good Christian book, or sit and listen to our pastor at church. We no longer have to "dig it out" for ourselves: all we need do is listen to someone else who has done the research for us. No sacrifice is necessary on our part to hear the truth of God, for it is readily available — even to those whose Christian lives consist of little more than weekly churchgoing.

I certainly appreciate the thousands of Christian schools that have sprung up across our country in the last ten to twenty years. Yet, more and more I have heard words of caution and alarm by those who have come to realize that some children brought up in Christian families and Christian schools have learned ABOUT God without ever really knowing him personally. Like parrots who have been taught to quote Bible verses, many children have learned the terminology but lack the reality.

RESCUING THE SECOND-GENERATION SAINTS

What can be done to keep our children

from the lukewarmness that comes from having a secondhand faith?

1. Probably the most important way is that we ourselves need to display an active, alive, enjoyable, and powerful relationship with the Lord. If we are lifeless, boring, compromised, stick- in-the-mud Christians we won't have much of an impact in telling our children they should be zealous followers of Jesus. Our example will have a much greater influence than our words.
2. We need to be serious about praying for our children and with our children. Peter's great revelation of who Jesus is seems to have come immediately after Jesus had been praying for the disciples, (Luke 9:18-20). No matter how good our example or our words, there is still a crucial need for the Lord Himself to work by His Spirit to deal with the hearts of our children, (John 16:7016; Ephesians 1:15-18).
3. Our children need to be in an atmosphere where they are frequently hearing the Word of God. Deuteronomy 6:4-9 instructs parents to diligently share the Lord's commandments with their children when they are sitting at home, walking down the road, lying down at night or getting up in the morning. Rather than being confined only to times of "family devotions," or "religious" times, the Word of God is supposed to be a natural part of our conversation in everything we do.
4. It is important that we don't get so wrapped up in pursuing our secular job, or even our ministry, that we neglect to spend quality time with our children. Many sincere Christians have become so busy serving people in the church, evangelizing or going to meetings, that their children end up resenting the God who seems to always be taking their parents away. This may be one of the reasons why the sons of Eli, the high priest, turned out to be immoral, rebellious men who did not know the Lord. (I Samuel 2:12, 22-25).
5. Use discretion about those with whom you allow your children to spend their time. "Bad company corrupts good morals" (I Corinthians 15:33). People tend to become like those with whom they associate. This "parental discretion" applies not only to your children's friends, but also to the television and movies they see, the music they listen to, and the books they read.
6. Despite the clear need to protect our children from destructive forces, it is also true that we can become overly protective so they never learn to make any decisions on their own, or stand in their own faith. I once heard about a newborn racoon that was found by some humans and taken in as a pet. The racoon grew up and one day escaped from the house, only to be killed by a nearby dog. Ordinarily a racoon is quite capable of defending itself, but this racoon had been spoiled by its soft environment and had never learned to fight. Likewise, we too must beware of keeping our children so sheltered and isolated that they never learn to depend on God and survive in the real world.

7. We need to find ways to encourage our children to exercise their spiritual gifts and find their ministries. Too often children are expected to be only spectators in spiritual things. However, constantly being a spectator eventually gets boring and tends to take away our incentive to seek God or be a part of the church. Our children need to grow up knowing they are important to God and that He can use them in witnessing, in encouraging others, in serving, and in supernatural spiritual manifestations.

It is God's intention that our children reach and **surpass** our level of fruitfulness! And yet this is not something that happens automatically or by wishful thinking. It begins as we pray that God will reveal Himself personally to our children and then that each of them would so see a vision for his life that he is willing to pay the price of "discipling himself for the purpose of godliness". (I Timothy 4:7). ■

Bob & Jim Buchan oversee FOCUS MINISTRIES, Box 15777 Columbus, Ohio 43215, a ministry devoted to the unity of the church in Ohio.

Elijah and the End Times continued from page 22

speak the same essential message, right out of the same text, and POW!—something would be loosed in my heart. I might not sleep much that night; and weeks, months, years later, that word would still be reverberating in my inner man. My attitudes, perceptions, speech, and conduct, my *life*, had been changed.

Life had gone forth from that speaker because the word of the Lord in *his* mouth was truth. I don't think that it became truth in him because he diligently did his Bible studies, knew how to use a concordance, was pretty sharp in speaking, and knew how to quote the right Scriptures and subscribe to the correct doctrines. There is no cheap, easy, or coldly mechanical way to become a fit vessel for eternal truth. There was more than a Bible study going on that day; there was a man who was dead and hid with Christ standing before God and God's people, and the same spirit Who raised that widow woman's son was freely pouring the waters of life into my own thirsty soul. ■

> For our gospel came not unto you in word only, but also in power, and in the Holy Ghost, and in much assurance; as ye know what manner of men we were among you for your sake (I Thessalonians 1:5)

Aaron (Art) Katz is the author of Ben Israel and REALITY: The Hope of Glory. For two decades, Aaron has been considered a voice of awakening to a sleeping church. Now his prophetic warnings have proven their validity and timeliness.

The Necessity of Prayer continued from page 32

be eaten, what shall be drunk, what shall be worn. Faith lives in the present, and regards the day as being sufficient unto the evil thereof. It lives day by day, and dispels all fears for the morrow. Faith brings great ease of mind and perfect peace of heart.

> "Thou wilt keep him in perfect peace whose mind is stayed on Thee: because he trusted in Thee."

When we pray, "Give us this day our daily bread," we are, in a measure, shutting tomorrow out of our prayer. We do not live in tomorrow but in today. We do not seek tomorrow's grace or tomorrow's bread. They thrive best, and get most out of life, who live in the present. They pray best who pray for today's needs, not for tomorrow's, which may render our prayers unnecessary and redundant by not existing at all!

True prayers are born of present trials and present needs. Bread, for today, is bread enough. Bread given for today is the strongest sort of pledge that there will be bread tomorrow. Victory today, is the assurance of victory tomorrow. Our prayers need to be focused upon the present. We must trust God today, and leave the morrow entirely with Him. The present is ours; the future belongs to God. Prayer is the task and duty of each reoccurring day daily prayer for daily needs.

As every day demands its bread, so every day demands its prayer. No amount of praying, done today, will suffice for tomorrow's praying. On the other hand, no praying for tomorrow is of any great value to us today. Today's manna is what we need; tomorrow God will see that our needs are supplied. This is the faith which God seeks to inspire. So leave tomorrow, with its cares, its needs, its troubles, in God's hands. There is no storing tomorrow's grace or tomorrow's praying; neither is there any laying-up of today's grace, to meet tomorrow's necessities. We cannot have tomorrow's grace, we cannot eat tomorrow's bread, we cannot do tomorrow's praying. "Sufficient unto the day is the evil thereof;" and, most assuredly, if we possess faith, sufficient also, will be the good. ■

The Church and the Kingdom continued from page 15

certainly fail in fulfilling God's will. We often look to the Old Testament and Moses as our role model for pastors when he was in fact meant to be a model of Jesus who is the Deliverer. When Jesus ascended He gave *gifts*, not *a* gift, back to His church.

Instead of giving one man, He gave a multiplicity of gifts signifying that the leadership would be a team leadership and not an individual. This team, submitting to one another and listening to the voice of Jesus, the Head, will be able to convey to the rest of the body the message that will keep the body in health and in tune with the overall purpose of God.

It is apparent that in the infinite wisdom and ingenuity of God He did not leave just one form of government for the church. The only absolute rule is that Jesus is the Head and has absolute authority to make all of the decisions. God is infinitely diverse in His entire creation. He makes every snowflake different, He makes every person different, and He makes every congregation different. Regardless of whether a group of people choose democratic rule, eldership rule, or some other rule, mutual submission to the anointing and to the gifts that He has given to men must be the order if kingdom structure is to be followed. ■

Dudley Hall is president of Successful Christian Living Ministries in Euless, Texas. He and his brother T.D. are committed to a ministry of revival, renewal, restoration and awakening. A graduate of Samford University, Dudley has been a pastor, conference speaker and internationally recognized teacher to the body of Christ.

Discovering Your Destiny continued from page 28

> Be completely humble and gentle, be patient, bearing with one another in love (Ephesians 4:2).
>
> Be kind and compassionate to one another, forgiving each other, just as in Christ, God forgave you (Ephesians 4:3).

There is probably no area of life where it is more difficult to obey Biblical truth than in broken and difficult relationships. We are taught in the Bible to love our enemies and pray for those who persecute us (Luke 6:32-26; Matthew 5:46). If we are offended by someone, it is God's will for us to forgive them, and to keep on forgiving until we are healed of the hurt sustained in the relationship and we freely forgive them. We must choose to love the person we are offended by with God's love as an act of obedience and faith.

Some relationships come easy, and others have to be worked at. Love and unity do not happen by accident. It is a result of making the right choices over and over again. If we are involved in a destructive relationship, one that is damaging us emotionally or physically, God does not expect us to continue endlessly to expose ourselves to a harmful relationship. But even if we withdraw from a person because it is too painful, God still wants us to forgive them. By forgiving, we release bitterness from our lives and rise above the others person's faults and weaknesses (Proverbs 15:17-18, 14:7).

As we love and forgive one another, God's love is released into our lives and it becomes a powerful witness to the reality of His presence in our life. The preceding ten points are the will of God for each of us. Before God can use us or give us 'special assignments' He has to know if we can be trusted with what He has already given us. If we want to us used by God and enter into the destiny He has for our life, we must first take care of these basics. ■

---

*Floyd McClung is the International Executive Director of Youth With A Mission and the founder of the International Center for Urban Missions. He is the author of nine challenging and insightful books including: **Intimacy With God**, **Effective Evangelism**, **The Father Heart of God** and **Holiness and the Spirit of the Age** (his most recent release). Floyd has become known as a leader who combines a radical commitment to Jesus and biblical Christianity with patience for the lost, tolerance for Christians of different persuasions and integrity in His own walk.*

Bible Studies For A Firm Foundation

by Bob & Rose Weiner

The following is an excerpt from a comprehensive study by the same title which comes in a high quality 8 1/2 x 11 book which is distributed by MorningStar (see Order Form in the back) and Bob & Rose Weiner Ministries, P.O. Box 1799, Gainsville, FL 32602. The answers are located on page 62 .

BAPTISM IN WATER

When we come to Jesus and repent of our sins, we enter into what the Bible calls the "born again" experience. We experience a "new birth" and receive a new heart. Jesus comes to dwell in our hearts by faith. We become partakers of eternal life, for eternal life is in the Son. When we depart from this life, we shall go to be with the Lord.

1. What are three vital elements of the Christian life? (Acts 2:38)
   a.
   b.
   c.

In our previous studies we have discussed the atonement of Jesus and God's provision for man's sins. We have discussed what true repentance and submission to the Lordship of Jesus means. We come now to our next truth, water baptism, in which we experience a burial of our old nature and a rising to walk with Christ in newness of life. Water baptism in itself is not effectual for salvation.

2. What did Jesus Himself say? (Matt. 28:19)

Let us now examine additional Scriptures concerning the significance of water baptism.

3. For what purpose was our old sin-loving nature crucified with Him? (Rom 6:6)
   a.
   b.

> *"We know that our old (unrenewed) self was nailed to the cross with Him in order that (our) body, (which is the instrument) of sin, might be made ineffective and inactive for evil, that we might no longer be the slaves of sin."*
>
> *—Rom. 6:6 (Amplified Version)*

4. What provision did Jesus make for the putting off of the sin-loving nature? (Col. 2:11)

5. What is the circumcision of Christ? (Col. 2:11-12)

This circumcision, made without hands, is a supernatural work of God. In a sense, in the waters of baptism, God supernaturally takes His scalpel and cuts away from our life the bondage to sin and buries it. A tremendous deliverance and victory takes place.

6. What was circumcision a sign of under the Old Covenant? (Gen. 17:10-11)

7. What happened to those who were not circumcised and why? (Gen. 17:13-14)
   a.
   b.

8. With whom did God establish this covenant of circumcision? (Gen. 17:19)

9.From whom are we descended as the children of promise? (Rom. 9:6-8)

10. Whom did Paul say were the true circumcision? (Phil. 3:3)

11. How did Moses, prophetically speaking of the New Covenant, describe this true circumcision? (Deut. 30:6)

Let us look at another Old Testament example. After forty years of wandering, the generation of disobedient Israelites, whom God had originally brought out of Egypt, died in the wilderness. When the Lord rolled back the waters of the Jordan River just as He had done at the Red Sea, this new generation walked through the Jordan River and into the promised land.

12. What was the first thing that they did? (Josh. 5:2)

13. Why did they do it? (Josh. 6:5-7)

14. What did the Lord say that He did when they were circumcised? (Josh. 5:9)

Before the Israelites could go up and possess the promised land, they had to be circumcised so that the reproach of Egypt might be rolled away from them. That circumcision was a sign in their flesh of their covenant with God. So also, under the New Covenant before we can go up and possess our promised inheritance, we must receive the circumcision of Jesus, made without hands, in putting off the "body of the sins of the flesh". Through this circumcision we are uprooted from the world, of which Egypt is a picture, and the reproach of the world is rolled away from us.

15. What then is circumcision in the New Covenant? (Col. 2:11-13)

Circumcision in the natural sense is the cutting away of the unclean part, the foreskin of the man. In the spiritual sense, circumcision of a cutting away of the whole body of sins, the sin-loving nature. Even more, baptism is a burial and resurrection, a total dying of the old self by union with Christ, a real and present rising again by participation in His risen life.

Another beautiful picture of water baptism is found in the Old Testament. It is a type and shadow of the meaning of baptism under the New Covenant. The Israelites had been held in bondage in Egypt for many years. They had been enslaved to Pharaoh, the cruel king. When the Lord brought them forth from bondage in the Exodus, He parted the Red Sea before them. The water was like a wall on either side of them as the Israelites passed through to the other side. Pharaoh and his armies, who were pursuing Israel, followed them into the water. The Lord, however, caused the water to roll back together cutting the Egyptians off and causing them to drown.

The ones who held Israel in bondage and slavery in Egypt, who were pursuing her in her new relationship with God, were buried in the waters of the Red Sea. Israel was left alone on the other side of the water free from slavery, free to be servants of their God. If the sea had not buried the

Egyptians, the threat of slavery would have followed them into the promised land. Not only would Israel have had to fight her enemies in the promised land, but she would have had to fight the one who was trying to bring her back into bondage. Those who have come to faith in Christ and are identified with Him through water baptism have been made free from the power and bondage of sin and have pressed on into the promised land able to meet and conquer their enemies head on.

16. In fact, what does Paul say about Israel's experience at the Red Sea? (I Cor. 10:1-2)

17. When believers are baptized, they are following Jesus in what experience of His? (Rom. 6:4)
   a.
   b.

18. If we have been united with Him in the likeness of His death, what shall we also be? (Rom. 6:5)

19. Jesus partook of our flesh and blood and died. Why did He do this? (Heb. 2:14-15)
   a.
   b.

As He hung on the cross, Jesus became sin on our behalf (II Cor. 5:21). The purpose of this was to bring us to God the Father. Jesus died on the cross to make a perfect atonement for man's sinful and lost condition. On the third day He arose from the dead and triumphed over Satan, thereby providing for man's salvation. Because we receive His life when we make Jesus Lord, our relationship to God is made alive and we also live in fellowship with God. Likewise, as we partake in water baptism, we share Jesus' burial and resurrection. Because we now share the resurrection life of Jesus, sin no longer has dominion over us.

Now that we have established the Scriptural meaning of baptism, let us look into the Scriptural application of it.

20. How did the people act who received the Word of God? (Acts 2:41)

21. What did the people of Samaria do after they believed Philip's teaching? (Acts 8:12)

22. What did the Ethiopian eunuch desire after he had heard the message of Philip about the Messiah? (Acts 8:35-36)

23. In what way, or by what method, was the eunuch baptized? (Acts 8:38-39)

The baptisms throughout the New Testament, including the baptisms of John, were all done by immersion — the people all went down into the water and came up again. The water represents the grave where the burial takes place.

24. What did the Philippian jailer do after believing Paul's message? (Acts 16:29-33)

25. When was he baptized? (Acts 16:33)

26. When were those who heard Peter's message baptized? (Acts 2:41)

Notice the immediacy of all the baptisms recorded in the book of Acts. Likewise, there should be no delay in the baptism of believers today.

27. In what name did Jesus tell the disciples to baptize? (Matt. 28:19)

28. In what name did the disciples baptize? (Acts 2:38; Acts 8:14-16; Acts 10:45-48; Acts 19:5)

We read in Colossians 2:9: "For in Him all the fulness of Deity in bodily form." Jesus' disciples understood this; for having His command, they went everywhere baptizing new believers. They were baptizing in the name which is above all names, in the name which all authority of heaven and earth is invested, and that name is Jesus. In the name of Jesus, demons are cast out, the sick are healed, and the lame walk.

29. Into whom are we baptized? (Rom. 6:3)

30. Many believers have gone through the motions of baptism, yet have not experienced a genuine New Testament baptism. What have they experienced? (Acts 19:3-4)

In the Old Testament, an account is given of Naaman, the captain of the army of the King of Syria, who had leprosy. He went to Elisha, the prophet of God, to ask for healing. Leprosy in the Scripture is a type of the "body of sins of the flesh" or of the bondage of the power of sin because there is no cure for this disease apart from the mercy of God. the whole flesh is infected, and the end of it is death.

31. What did Elisha tell him to do? (II Kings 5:9-10)

32.What was his response? (II Kings 5:11-12)

Likewise, many people are insulted by God's command for water baptism, thinking it is silly and ridiculous.

33. What was the servant's advice to him, and what did he do? (II Kings 5:13-14)

Likewise, we must become as little children and obey the simple things that God asks us to do. His ways are far above our ways. We must lean not to our own understanding. We must be careful lest we only desire to do great feats for God yet are not willing to humble ourselves to God's way of doing things.

MEMORY VERSE: Col. 2:11-12

BAPTISM IN THE HOLY SPIRIT

1. What instruction did Peter give to the Jewish people who were under conviction following his sermon at Pentecost? (Acts 2:37-38)
   a.
   b.
   c.

2. What did Jesus tell His disciples to do before they went out into the world to preach repentance? (Luke 24:47-53)

3. What was the "promise of the Father" they were to receive? (Acts 1:4-5)

4. What did Jesus say would happen when the Holy Spirit came upon them? (Acts 1:8)

Notice that this empowering produces the ability to be a witness; that is, it gives the ability to live the Christian life and the power to preach the gospel.

5. How did Jesus fulfill His ministry? (Acts 10:38)

6. What type of proof had the disciples been given of Jesus' resurrection? (Acts 1:3)

It is interesting to notice that although the disciples had been taught by Jesus over a period of three years, had seen the resurrected Messiah in all His glory and power over a period of 40 days, and had fellowshipped intensely with Him, they were not allowed to go and preach the Gospel until after they had received the baptism of the Holy Spirit and have been clothed with power from on High. Yet, how many "born again" believers attempt to go and preach the Gospel without it?

7. What did Jesus say about the Holy Spirit that He would send? (John 14:16-17)

8. What are two other named for the Holy Spirit? (John 14:16-17)
   a.
   b.

9. What other things did Jesus tell the disciples that the Holy Spirit would do for them? (John 14:26; John 15:26; John 16:13)
   a.
   b.
   c.
   d.
   e.

10. Paul also speaks of this empowering. What did he say about the Gospel which he preached? (I Cor. 2:4)

11. On what should the faith of men not rest? (I Cor. 2:5)

12. On what should their faith rest? (I Cor. 2:5)

13. How did Paul say that we might know the things that God has given us? (I Cor. 2:9-12)

14. What did Jesus say the Spirit would do for us when we are delivered up before the governors, kings and those in authority? (Matt. 10:18-20)

15. Consequently, what are we exhorted to do when we are delivered up for the defense of the Gospel? (Matt. 10:19)

16. What are two other names for the Holy Spirit? (Matt. 10:20; Gal. 4:6)
   a.
   b.

All these benefits are available to all believers when the Holy Spirit is received.

17. Besides the eleven apostles, who else was waiting to receive the promise of the Holy Spirit? (Acts 1:13-15)

18. What was the total number present? (Acts 1:15)

19. Although these people were staying in the upper room for lodging purposes, where were they continually meeting to praise the Lord? (Luke 24:52-53)

20. During this time, because of the Feast of Pentecost, who was present at Jerusalem and in the temple? (Acts 2:5)

21. What happened when the Holy Spirit was given? (Acts 2:1-4)
    a.
    b.
    c.

22. What happened when this sound occurred? (Acts 2:6)

This out-pouring of the Holy Spirit did not take place in a small room somewhere behind locked doors. This thing was not done in a corner but in the temple before the eyes of all Israel.

23. How did Peter explain what was happening? (Acts 2:14-21)

24. What did the tongues of fire that rested upon the believers represent? (Matt. 3:11-12)

This fire of the Holy Spirit represents the cleansing and purifying work of the Spirit in the lives of believers.

25. How does John describe this cleansing work? (Matt. 3:12)

26. The prophet Malachi speaks of these cleansing fires. Describe this refining and purifying work that is to be done by the Holy Spirit. (Mal. 3:1-3)

This cleansing and purifying work does not take place overnight. It is a process like that of a smelter. A refiner of silver heats the silver over a burning fire. As the silver becomes hot, all the dross and impurities rise to the top. He then skims them off. He continues heating and skimming off the dross again and again until he can see his image reflected clearly in the silver. So also the Holy Spirit through the trials and tests skims all the dross and impurities from our lives that the image of Jesus may be seen in us.

27. In fact, what does Paul say the Spirit of the Lord has come to do? (II Cor. 3:18)

28. How did the Gentiles receive the Holy Spirit? (Acts 10:44-45)

29. How did they know the Gentiles had received the Holy Spirit? (Acts 10:45-46)

30. How did the believers at Samaria receive the Holy Spirit? (Acts 8:17)

31. How did the believers at Ephesus receive the Holy Spirit? (Acts 19:6)

32. What happened when they received the Holy Spirit? (Acts 19:6)

33. What does the prophet Ezekiel say about the Holy Spirit when he is prophesying about the New Covenant? (Ezk. 36:26-27)

34. To whom is the promised gift of the Holy Spirit made available? (Acts 2:39)

35. To whom will the Father give the Holy Spirit? (Luke 11:13)

MEMORY VERSE: Acts 2:38-39

Preparation For Ministry

Part II

by Rick Joyner

Each part to this series is a complete study by itself and it is not necessary to have taken the previous studies to benefit from it.

The foundation of all ministry is the character of the Holy Spirit. He is "the Helper", He prays for us, leads us into all truth, testifies of Jesus and convicts the world of sin. As vessels for the Holy Spirit these functions help define the purpose of our ministry.

We can see in these functions the ministries of the Pastor (helper), the Teacher (leading us to truth), the Evangelist (testifying of Jesus), and the Prophet (convicting the world of sin). All of these are found in the apostolic ministry, which is basically a composite of the others. As all ministry is founded upon our calling to be priests unto the Lord, these are also founded upon the Holy Spirit's ministry of praying for us.

Even though each aspect of the Holy Spirit's functions may be represented in a specific ministry, if we have the Holy Spirit we should manifest all of these to some degree. Let's look at each one of these individually and then see how they fit together.

THE PASTOR

("Helper")

When the One whose nature is to be "the Helper" begins to lead our life we begin to reflect His nature; we will just want to help people. Because the Holy Spirit is the Helper He is compelled by His nature to get involved in people's needs. Those who live by the Spirit will be the same way.

Though the church has had a tendency to relegate the ministry of "helps" to projects like cutting the grass and washing the dishes, the basic nature of this ministry is spiritual; it is, after all, the Holy *Spirit* who gives this ministry. The true ministry of helps is the foundation for the pastor ministry. What is the cry of a drowning man? "Help!" Answering the desperate cries for help is the basic function of the ministry of helps, which of course is the basic function of the pastor.

The true nature of the ministry of helps, as it is restored to the church, will be one of the primary tools used to break down the divisions and bringing unity to the body of Christ. When someone saves your life there is a lifelong bond to that person that will transcend just about any kind of pressure put upon the relationship. The same is true when someone saves your spiritual life. Churches that are drowning are going to be saved by other congregations who respond to their needs instead of waiting like hungry vultures to devour the body. It will take but a few such actions to begin convicting the rest of the church of its most unchristian behavior toward the rest of the body of Christ. When this true ministry of helps is restored it will quickly result in a profound restoration of true spiritual health to the whole church.

It is the nature of our Shepherd to leave the ninety-nine sheep who are doing well to go after the one who has strayed. When the pastor ministry is fully restored we will again see genuine concern and reaching out to those congregations and individuals who have strayed from the way, instead of the present tendency to attack and banish them. It is the nature of the Holy Spirit to seek and to help those who are lost, not afflict and condemn them.

THE TEACHER

(to lead into all truth)

Another basic function of the Holy Spirit is to lead us into all truth. This function is specifically manifested in the ministry of the **Teacher.** There is far more to the teaching ministry than just the ability to expound biblical doctrine accurately, or articulately; the true teacher does not only impart truth *but also imparts a love for the truth.*

Just having truth will not keep us from deception, but it is the believer who has a love for the truth who will walk in truth. We can know all doctrines accurately and still be deceived; deception is not just misunderstanding doctrine, it is not being in God's will. We can memorize the Bible and not know the truth. Truth is not just a matter of getting our facts lined up right; the Truth is a Person.

There is an ancient proverb which states, "You can give a man a fish and he has one meal; if you teach him how to fish he can feed himself for the rest of his life." The goal of the Teacher is not to just impart the word, but to impart a passion for the word.

This is not to imply that we do not want to be utterly devoted to accuracy of doctrine. If we are going to love the truth we certainly want it to be factual, but we will never be solidly established in truth until we esteem a love for truth above a love for facts. When the Holy Spirit was sent to lead us into the truth He came to do it by imparting His nature, not just principles and formulas. The best hermeneutics in the world will be useless unless we are walking by the Spirit. Biblical truth is not derived by having the proper formula but by the revelation of the Spirit. It is only by the Holy Spirit that anyone ever comes to the truth. No one can come to the Father unless the Son reveals Him, and no one can come to the Son unless the Father draws him. Proper hermeneutics can be helpful in keeping a seeker safely away from the precipice of free association and speculation, but is not the foundation for seeking the truth. That foundation is our love for the Son, who is the Truth, and our openness to the guidance of the Holy Spirit.

THE EVANGELIST

(to testify of Jesus)

Another fundamental aspect of the Holy Spirit's ministry is to testify of Jesus, which is basically the ministry of the Evangelist.

Like the other ministries, the authority of the evangelist is based on love—foremost, a love for the Lord. Anyone who has ever "fallen in love" remembers well how his every thought was somehow influenced by a passion for the object of their affections. If we have retained our first love with Jesus it will be the same way; every thought and action will be influenced by our passion for Him. True evangelism is the overflow of our love for the Lord and what He has done for us.

The scripture testifies that all things were made through Jesus and for Him and in Him all things will be summed up. In everything that was created the Father was looking for His Son. The ultimate Purpose of the creation is to be conformed to the image of the Son. The Holy Spirit could actually be called the Personification of the love the Father has for His Son, and the Power of that love. When we receive the Holy Spirit He releases that same love for the Son in us. There is nothing in this world more powerful or more contagious that the Passion for the Son of God. There is no one in this world more contagious that the one who is drawing closer to Jesus; everyone around them will sooner or later become infected. True evangelism is not a formula or practiced procedure developed to evoke a certain commitment from people; it is simply the spreading of that love for the Son.

This is not to say that a commitment to the Lord is not required for conversion; certainly it is! But how much of our evangelism has not been more devoted to converting others to our doctrines, churches, programs, even our pastors, almost anything but to the Lord Himself. There is only one foundation that can be laid: Jesus Christ (I Corinthians 3:11). A conversion built upon anything else could be a false conversion.

Because God is love all true ministry is based first upon love. All true conversions begin with love. When we see Jesus we will love Him, and then we will feel remorse for our sin and abhor anything which offends Him, out of our love, not from a religious spirit.

True evangelism testifies of Jesus and His love for us through the cross; that is enough. That is the Power of God as revealed through the Holy Spirit and declared by Paul:

> And when I came to you, brethren, I did not come with superiority of speech or of wisdom, proclaiming to you the wisdom of God.
>
> For I determined to know nothing among you except Jesus Christ, and Him crucified.
>
> And I was with you in weakness and in fear and in much trembling.
>
> And my message and my preaching were not in persuasive words of wisdom, but in demonstration of the Spirit and of power,
>
> that your faith should not rest on the wisdom of men but on the power of God (I Corinthians 2:1-5).

Because the gospel message seems foolish to the natural men we are trying to win, we often are tempted to embellish it to make it more acceptable. This temptation is the same one used to seduce our first parents in the garden; the Tree of Knowledge can still seem more appealing than the Tree of Life. **"But I am afraid, lest as the serpent deceived Eve by His craftiness, your minds should be led astray from the simplicity and purity of devotion to Christ" (II Corinthians 11:3).**

If we start with a wrong foundation, a conversion built upon a foundation other than the Person of Jesus, our entire spiritual life will be distorted until we have relaid the proper foundation in our life. It is not the work of the evangelist to build the house of our faith, but it is his commission to start the foundation properly.

THE PROPHET

(to convict the world of sin)

It is a (not "the") primary commission of

the prophetic ministry to stand uncompromisingly against sin. This is, of course, a reflection of the Holy Spirit's ministry of convicting the world of sin. But how does the prophetic ministry do this? Both the church and the world are weary of the critical spirit which masquerades as the prophetic mandate to bring conviction. G. Campbell Morgan once observed:

> There may be right things done in a wrong spirit. I seldom find men strenuously fighting what they are pleased to call heterodox teaching, and in bitter language denouncing false doctrine, without being more afraid for the men denouncing than for the men denounced. There is an anger against impurity which is impure. There is a zeal for orthodoxy which is most unorthodox. There is a spirit that contends for the faith which is in conflict with faith. If men have lost their first love, they will do more harm than good by their defense of the faith.
>
> Behind the denunciation of sin there must always be the tenderness of first love if that denunciation is not to become evil in its bitterness. Behind zeal for truth, there must always be the spaciousness of first love if that zeal is not to become narrowed into hate. There have been men who have become so self-centered in a narrowness that they are pleased to designate as holding the truth, that the very principle for which they contend has been excluded from their life and service. All zeal for the Master that is not the outcome of love to Him is worthless.

This is not to imply that all who are ministering in the prophetic, or who are preaching against sin, are doing it in a critical spirit. Unfortunately, those who preach with a critical spirit muddy the waters for those who are simply trying to bring the necessary correction in a godly manner. It is not enough to have an understanding of what it wrong; there is a spiritual grace that is essential when bringing correction if a believer to use the truth to set men free instead of merely increasing their burdens.

It is apparent that each of these ministries named must use certain emphases of the other ministries to fulfill their own purpose. A true evangelist will have a portion of the prophet's anointing to convict of sin, a measure of the pastor's anointing to counsel the disoriented, and some of the teacher's ability to bring enlightenment. The prophet must also have the compassion of the pastor, the zeal of the teacher for doctrinal accuracy and the heart of the evangelist for the lost. Balance is not compromise, it is the grace that makes truth liberation instead of bondage.

The prophetic ministry has just as much responsibility to walk in the fruit of the Spirit as anyone else in the body. Concerning his calling to bring conviction for sin, it is essential that the prophet not become reactionary, bitter and frustrated. Frustration is not a fruit of the Spirit and if we try to bring conviction in the spirit of frustration it will increase the power of the sin. If we are not ministering in the Holy Spirit we will minister the Law and **"the power of sin is the law" (I Corinthians 15:56).** The law uses external pressure to change outward behavior while leaving the heart mired in corruption and deception. The aim of the Spirit is to change the heart, which sometimes takes a while to manifest itself in outward behavior.

This is why the primary calling is to bring conviction for *sin*, not *sins*. If we are going to bring true conviction we must know one another after the spirit, not the flesh. A parrot can learn to say and do the right things, but it will never be in its heart. Prophetic frustration comes when we are in fact being very unprophetic, looking at the externals from the human perspective instead of seeing from God's perspective. When we start seeing as God does we will begin to see an exceedingly great army in the most dry bones! We will not just run around telling the bones how dry they are, we will begin to prophesy life to the bones!

All ministry is a reflection of Jesus' own ministry. We can see His manner in bringing correction to the seven churches in the Book of Revelation. He first encouraged each church, then He addressed their problems, then He gave them a promise of what they would receive after they had overcome them. He addressed their sins directly but surrounded this with a great deal of encouragement and hope. ■

QUESTIONS:

1. What is the foundation of all true ministry?

2. The Holy Spirit was sent to be the "Helper," to lead us into truth, to testify of Jesus and to convict the world of sin. Which of the equipping ministries of Ephesians chapter four relates to each of these aspects of His purpose?

3. What primary ministry is the foundation of the pastor's ministry?

4. Is it right for the pastor to be more concerned about one hurting person than a multitude who are healthy?

5. What is the essence of the true teaching ministry?

6. Can biblical truth be derived from having the right formula for exegesis?

7. What is the anointing of the evangelist primarily based upon?

8. Why did the apostle Paul refrain from using superior speech or (human) wisdom when presenting the gospel?

9. What is all true spiritual authority based upon?

10. What is all ministry a reflection of?

Turn to page 62 for answers to these questions.

ACCOUNTANT

John A. Franklin, C.P.A.
2101 Sardis Rd. N., Suite 220
Charlotte, NC 28227
(704) 845-1195

ARCHITECT

Miller, Moore, Mayne Architects & Assoc., P.A.
P.O. Box 1224
112 Honeysuckle Rd.
Dothan, AL 36302
(205) 793-7386

ART

Graphic Art

Seward's Ad Art
Blanton Seward
5428 Dorchester Road
Richmond, VA 23225
(804) 780-0588

Prints

Delores Roberson
419 Domar Dr.
Townsend, TN 37882
(615) 448-6737

ATTORNEY

Jackie O. Isom
P.O. Box 369
Hamilton, AL 35570
(205) 921-7488

AUDIO SYSTEMS

AcousTech
Roland E. Dutzmann
8254 Ames Way
Arvada, CO 80003
(303) 429-4912

BOOKS

Book Binder

Cary Peck
4295 Darley Ave.
Boulder, CO 80303
(303)499-4373

CHURCHES

Belmont Church
Don Finto
68 Music Square East
Nashville, TN 37203
(615) 256-2123

Covenant Bible Church
Charles Brown, Pastor
P.O. Box 654
Lincolnton, NC 28093
(704) 735-1559

Denver Vineyard Christian Fellowship
Tom Stipe, Pastor
9725 W. 50th Ave.
Wheatridge, CO 80033

Lifespring Church
Randall Worley, Pastor
P.O. Box 759
Pineville, NC 28134
(704) 542-9951

Metro Vineyard Fellowship
Mike Bickle, Pastor
11610 Grandview Rd.
Kansas City, MO 64137

New Heart Covenant Church
Bob Daniel, Pastor
1700 Progress Lane
Charlotte, NC 28205
(704) 535-3337

Resurrection Lutheran Church
2825 Shenandoah Ave.
Charlotte, NC 28205
(704) 377-6575

Restoration Church
Doug White, Pastor
90 Wilshire Village Hwy. 10
Euless, TX 76040
(817) 354-8500

Sojourn Church
Terry Moore, Pastor
3440 Sojourn Dr. #240
Carrollton, TX 75006
(214) 248-2912

COMPUTERS

Data Processing Consultants

Computers For Business
William E. Bennett
2843 Pembroke Rd.
Hollywood, FL 33020
(305) 920-9604

Software

Hermeneutika Bible Software Co.
Mark Rice
P.O. Box 98563
Seattle, WA 98198
(800) 55-BIBLE (Orders)
(206) 824-3927 (Information)

CONSTRUCTION

Construction Materials Testing

Earth Materials Testing Co., Inc.
Rt. 3, Box 130
Arkadelphia, AR 71923
(501) 246-7225

Electric

Visak Electric, Inc.
3052 100th Place
Highland, IN 46322
(219) 924-6396

CONTRACTOR

General Contractor

Shalom Homes
Steve Kobernik
7450 Via Deldene
Highland, CA 92346
(714) 864-0726

COUNSELING

Marriage/Family

Dr. Harold Hammond
9009 Rouen Lane
Potomac, MD 20854
(301) 983-0532

Psychotherapy

Dr. Sandra Joy K. Bowen
8303 Arlington Blvd.
Fairfax, VA 22031
(703) 573-9186

DENTIST

Herbert S. Woodward, III
325 Elm Ave., Suite, A-2
Carlsbad, CA 92008
(619)729-7901

FINANCIAL SERVICES

Investment Advisor

Carolina Investment Advisors
R. Graham Pitt
P.O. Box 112
Shelby, NC 28150
(704) 481-0101

Nuismer, Fox & Co., Inc.
N. Jack Nuismer, Jr.
2103 Crestmoor Rd.
Nashville, TN 37215
(615) 298-3699

Investment Management

Daniels Financial Services, Ltd.
Paul R. Daniels, C.F.A.
17 Union Circle
Wheaton, IL 60187
(708) 653-5321

MINISTRY

Bible Teacher/Evangelist

Bill Lopez
P.O. Box 4204
Canyon Lake, CA 92380

Ministry Schools

Emmaus Road Ministry School
P.O. Box 400213
Euless, TX 76040
(817) 545-0282

Pinecrest Bible Training Center
Wade Taylor, President
P.O. Box 320
Salisbury Center, NY 13454

Music

Galestorm Productions
John G. Elliott, Director
P.O. Box 121474
Nashville, TN 37212

Pastor/Evangelist

Rev. Bernard Wright
7015 Glenview Dr.
Tampa, FL 33619
(813) 620-1865

Prophetic Ministry

Network of Prophetic Ministries
Bill Hamon, President
Route 2, Box 351
Pt. Washington, FL 34254

Other Ministry

Bob & Rose Weiner Ministries
P.O. Box 1799
Gainesville, FL 32602

Christian Retreats
Gerald Derstine, Director
Route 2, Box 279
Bradenton, FL 34202

Dimensions Ministries
Jack Taylor, Director
P.O. Box 6369
Ft. Worth, TX 76115

Erskin Holt Ministries
37 Corvilla Dr.
Zephyrhills, FL 33599

Focus Ministries
Bob & Jim Buchan, Directors
P.O. Box 15777
Colombus, OH 43212

James Robison Evangelistic Assoc.
P.O. Box 18489
Ft. Worth, TX 76118

Jerusalem Watch
Progressive Vision International
P.O. 31393
Jersalem, Israel 91313
02-2-80727

Mahesh Chavda Ministries
P.O. Box 24133
Ft. Lauderdale, FL 33307
(305) 462-3778

New Day Ministries
John Hamrick
3149 Colorado Dr. SW
Powder Springs, GA 30073
(404) 943-1221

Progressive Vision International
Tom Hess
117 Second St., NE #1
Washington, DC 20002
(202) 543-1172

Strategic Christian Services
Dennis Peacocke, Director
1221 Farmers Lane, Suite B
Santa Rosa, CA 95405
(707) 578-7700

Successful Christian Living Ministries
Dudley Hall, President
P.O. Box 101
Euless, TX 76039
(817) 267-9224

Youth

Youth of Destiny
Mike Kell, Director
P.O. Box 1665
Matthews, NC 28106
(704) 522-7028

PHYSICIAN

Chiropractic

Cornerstone Chiropractic Center
Dr. Darryl L. Fong
Dr. Cynthia C. Mitchell
1145 N. Lemon
Anaheim, CA 92801
(714) 776-3041

Karr Clinic
Dr. John A. Karr, D.C.
2105 E. 15th St.
Tulsa, OK 74104
(918) 744-0072

Dr. Jerry Lalla
2353 Rice St., Suite 210
Roseville, MN 55113
(612) 484-8521

PRINTERS

PIP Printing
Bob Petty
888 Highway 29 N
Concord, NC 28025
(704) 788-8400

PUBLISHING

Destiny Image Publishers
P.O. Box 351
Shippensburg, PA 17257

Strang Communications
Stephen Strang, Publisher
600 Rinehart Rd.
Lake Mary, FL 32746
(407) 333-0600

Desktop Publishing
Dynamic Resources
Heidi Haas
4184 N. Colony Blvd.
Dallas, TX 75056-3601
(214) 625-6071

READING PROGRAMS

Powerline Reading Programs
Donald L. Olson
P.O. Box 901778
Palmdale, CA 93590-1778
(800) 876-READ

WOODWORKING

Integrity Woodworking
Pat Selvey
34-09 41st St. 1-A
Long Island City, NY 11101
(718) 361-0535

NOTE: Business listings in this Directory are not necessarily endorsements by MorningStar Publications, the authors, or the editors.

See page 63 for ordering information.

See page 63 for ordering Information.

See page 63 for ordering Information.

ANSWERS:

Baptism in Water

1. a. Repent.
   b. Be baptized.
   c. Receive the Holy Spirit.

2. Make disciples of all nations and baptize them.

3. a. That our body of sin might be done away with.
   b. That we should no longer be slaves to sin.

4. By the circumcision of Christ.

5. Burial with Christ in baptism.

6. A sign of the covenant between God and Abraham and his descendants.

7. a. He was cut off from his people.
   b. He has broken God's covenant.

8. Isaac and his descendants.

9. Descendants of Isaac.

10. Those who worship in the Spirit and put no confidence in the flesh.

11. The circumcision of the heart.

12. They were all circumcised.

13. They had not been circumcised in the wilderness.

14. He had rolled away the reproach of Egypt from them.

15. Removal of the body of flesh by the circumcision of Christ.

16. They were baptized in the Sea.

17. a Burial.
   b. Resurrection.

18. In the likeness of His resurrection.

19. a. To render the devil powerless.
   b. To deliver those who were subject to slavery.

20. They were baptized.

21. They were baptized.

22. He desired baptism.

23. He went down into the water (immersion).

24. He was baptized.

25. Immediately.

26. The same day.

27. In the name of the Father, Son and Holy Spirit.

28. In the name of the Lord Jesus Christ.

29. We are baptized into Jesus Christ.

30. The baptism of repentance.

31. He told him to wash seven times in the Jordan.

32. He was furious and insulted.

33. If the prophet had told you to do some great thing, you would have done it. How much more should you do this simple thing. So Naaman washed and was cleansed.

Baptism in the Holy Spirit

1. a. Repent.
   b. Be baptized.
   c. Receive the Holy Spirit.

2. To wait in Jerusalem until they received the promise of the Father and were clothed with power from on High.

3. The baptism of the Holy Spirit.

4. They would receive power to be His witnesses.

5. Jesus fulfilled His ministry under the anointing of the Holy Spirit.

6. He presented Himself alive and by many convincing proofs appeared to them over a period of 40 days, speaking to them of things concerning the Kingdom of God.

7. He abides with you and shall be in you.

8. a. Helper or comforter.
   b. The Spirit of truth.

9. a. He will teach you all things.
   b. He will bring to your remembrance all the things that Jesus said.
   c. He will bear witness of Jesus.
   d. He will guide you into all truth.
   e. He will disclose to you what is to come.

10. His Gospel was not in persuasive words, but in the demonstration of the Spirit and of power.

11. It should not rest on the wisdom of men.

12. The power of God.

13. By the revelation of the Spirit.

14. He will give you what you shall speak.

15. Do not be anxious.

16. a. The Spirit of your Father.
   b. The Spirit of His Son.

17. The women, Mary the mother of Jesus, His brothers.

18. 120

19. In the temple.

20. Jews from every nation under heaven.

21. a. There came from heaven a noise like a violent rushing wind that filled all the house.
   b. Tongues of fire appeared on them.
   c. They began to speak with tongues as the Spirit gave them utterance.

22. The multitude of Jews there gathered around them, each hearing them speak in their own language.

23. He explained it as the outpouring of the Holy Spirit spoken of by the prophet Joel.

24. The baptism of fire.

25. he describes it as separating the wheat from the chaff, tossing it up continually until all impurities have been separated from the wheat.

26. The Lord will be like fuller's soap and a refiner's fire. He will purge and purify believers that they may offer unto the Lord offerings of righteousness.

27. To transform us into the same image of the Lord from glory to glory.

28. The Holy Spirit fell on them as they heard Peter's preaching.

29. They heard them speak with tongues and exalt God.

30. Through the laying on of hands.

31. Through the laying on of hands.

32. They spoke in tongues and prophesied.

33. I will put My Spirit within you and cause you to walk in My ordinances.

34. Unto you and your children and to all who are afar off, even as many as the Lord our God shall call.

35. To all His children who ask for it.

Preparation For Ministry

1. The character of the Holy Spirit.

2. Helper – pastor; Lead us into truth – teacher; Testify of Jesus – evangelist; Convict the world of sin – prophet.

3. The ministry of "helps."

4. Yes. It is the shepherd's nature to leave the ninety nine to go after the one who is lost. Therefore, true shepherds are seldom concerned with numbers as much as they are with the ones who are suffering.

5. To impart a love for the truth.

6. No. Biblical truth is not found by just having the right "formula" for biblical examination, but by being open to and following the Holy Spirit who was sent to lead us into all truth. (This is not to imply that using proper exegesis and hermeneutics are not helpful in keeping us on the right track.)

7. Loving Jesus from the heart. True evangelism is not technique or professionalism; living waters can only come from the innermost being. A heart overflowing with love for Jesus is the most contagious force on earth and will draw all men.

8. He maintained the simplicity of the cross as His message lest any be converted to anything or anyone but Jesus Himself.

9. Love. Without love we can do the right things in a wrong spirit and bring about the wrong result.

10. The ministry of Jesus.

CATALOG OF BOOKS & TAPES

Prices are valid through 6/30/91

Books

There Were Two Trees In The Garden
by Rick Joyner #RJ1-001 . . . . $5.95

The Harvest
by Rick Joyner #RJ1-002 . . . . $5.95

The Passover
by Rick Joyner #RJ1-003 . . . . $2.95

Leadership, Management, And The Five Essentials For Success
by Rick Joyner #RJ1-004 . . . . $5.95

Reality: The Hope Of Glory
by Aaron (Art) Katz #AK1-001 . . . . $5.95

The Three Battlegrounds
by Francis Frangipane #FF1-001 . . . $5.95

Holiness, Truth, And The Presence Of God
by Francis Frangipane #FF1-002 . . . $5.95

The Harvest Trilogy
by Rick Joyner & Robert Burnell
#MS1-001 . . . . $2.95

The Morning Star 1988–1989
#MS1-002 . . . . $5.00

Bible Studies For a Firm Foundation
by Bob & Rose Weiner #BW1-001 . . . $7.95

Books on Tape

Escape From Christendom (Burnell)
#MS7-001 (1 tape) $4.50

A Vision Of The Harvest (Joyner)
#MS7-002 (1 tape) $4.50

There Were Two Trees In The Garden (Joyner)
#MS7-003 (4 tapes) $17.50

The Harvest (Joyner)
#MS7-004 (4 tapes) $17.50

Reality: The Hope Of Glory (Katz)
#MS7-005 (5 tapes) $21.50

Holiness, Truth And The Presence Of God (Frangipane)
#MS7-006 (3 tapes) $13.50

The Three Battlegrounds (Frangipane)
#MS7-007 (3 tapes) $13.50

The Morning Star 1988-1989
#MS7-008 (3 tapes) $13.50

Music Tapes

Let All The Thirsty Come
By John G. Elliott

#JE6-001 (Cassette) $9.50
#JE6-002 (Compact Disk) $12.50

Coming Back
By Leonard Jones

#LJ6-001 (Cassette) $9.50

Subscriptions

The Morning Star "Tape Of The Month" (12 tapes)

#TM5-001 (US) $49.00
#FTM5-001 (Outside US) $59.00

The Morning Star Journal (1 year, 6 bi-monthly issues)

#MAG-001 (US) $10.00
#FMAG-001 (Outside US) $17.50

Professional Listings (1 year, 6 listings)
CBL-001 . . . . $35.00

ORDER FORM

Subscriber #____________

First Name ______ Initial ______ Last Name ______

Today's Date ___/___/___

Address ______

City ______ State ______ Zip (Required) ______

☐ Please send a complete book & tape catalog.

☐ Check here if change of address. (Enter old address below)

( ) ______ Daytime Phone #

CATALOG #	*QUANTITY*	*TITLE*	*COST EA.*	*TOTAL*
–				
–				
–				
–				
–				
–				
–				
–				

Sub Total	
Subscriber # ______ *10% Discount for Subscribers (REQUIRED)*	
Less Quantity Discount of ____*% (BOOKS ONLY)*	
NC Residents add 5% Sales Tax	
Shipping and Handling	
Donation to MorningStar Ministries	
TOTAL ENCLOSED	

Send to:

MorningStar Publications
P.O. Box 369
Pineville, North Carolina 28134

DISCOUNTS

Quanity Discounts are available for **book purchases only**. Any combination of titles may be used to quality for the discount. Discounts do not apply to tapes or special offers.

10 or more books	40% Discount
100 or more books	50% Discount
500 or more books	55% Discount
1000 or more books	60% Discount

SHIPPING & HANDLING

U.S. Shipping Rates

For orders < $10.00	1.50
$10.00 – $24.99	2.50
$25.00 – $49.99	3.50
$50.00 – $74.99	4.50
$75.00 – $99.99	5.50
$100.00 – $499.99	6% of total
$500.00 $999.99	5% of total
> $1,000.00	4% of total

International Shipping Rates

For orders < $10.00	2.50
$10.00 – $24.99	4.75
$25.00 – $49.99	7.00
$50.00 – $74.99	9.25
$75.00 – $99.99	11.50
$100.00 $499.99	11% of total
> $500.00	10% of total

NOTE: We do not invoice; all orders should include payment. We will ship UPS C.O.D. for orders of $50.00 or more in the U.S. Payment for foreign orders must be made in U.S. funds routed through an American bank. Make checks payable to M.P.I. (MorningStar Publications, Inc.).